Get A Life! In the City® Chicago

The Ultimate Guide to Classes and Hobbies,

Sports and Fitness, Dating and Networking,

Volunteering, Relaxing and much more

in and around the Windy City

by

Sheena M. Jones

Every effort has been made by the author to ensure the accuracy of the information within this book. Since organizations, businesses, and clubs frequently move, restructure or go out of business, please contact the organizations directly for the most current information on offerings, schedules, and fees. In no way is the author affiliated with any of the organizations included herein, as an agent. Further, the author disclaims any warranties or guarantees, express or implied, regarding the quality of any product or service offered by those organizations.

First published by AuthorHouse 02/21/05

Second Edition published by Get A Life! In the City® 11/30/05

ISBN:0-9766589-0-9

Printed in the United States of America
Chicago, IL

Cover design by Mo Spondouris of Farm It Out
farmitout2mo@yahoo.com

Dedication

This book is dedicated to my parents Shirley and Bruce Jones, my "lil' brother" Amari, and my good friend Anissa Beard.

Mama, you are my strength.
Daddy, you are my heart.
Amari, you are my joy.

Anissa, you are the only person I know who not only has a life, but who has 9 of them. Get better soon.

Acknowledgements

I'd like to thank the following people for their love, support, and kind words throughout this book writing process:

Princess Burkert	*Yasmin Wilkinson*
Avery Crump	*Lisa Kyeremateng*
Rachel Greene	*Malene Minor*
Charles Ridgner	*Nanette Jones*
Vanessa Alcocer	*Jason Froebe*
Edjuana Ross	*Mariya Kutwal*
Stacie Wiggan	*Baindu Wilkinson*
Javonne Jennings	*Tabitha Arguelles*
Jessica Mayotte	*Kristy Patsis*
Allison Claybon	*Monica Sullivan*
Luana Sheets	*Stacie Jackson*
Chris Bartosik	*Pat Carbajal*
LaToya Hayward	*Kelly Zimmer*
Bart Fitzpatrick	*Leslie Heatherly*
Karen Bradley	*Rolinda Stevenson*

Kurt Moriwaki—Get A Life! In the City logo designer

Mo Spondouris—Cover and Book designer

My grandmother Willie B. Hayward

Doug Wallace my sweetheart

In the City!
TABLE OF *Contents*

Take a Class! In the City

Get Buff! In the City

Get Connected! In the City

Do Good! In the City

Chill Out! In the City:

Foreword
by Bart Fitzpatrick of Sports Monster

Where was this book in 1990?!

When I moved to Chicago in 1990, I was filled with excitement about moving to live in a big city. Chicago was cleaner, safer and friendlier than my hometown of Philadelphia and way more affordable than metropolitan New York where I moved after college. The Windy City had so many things to see and do and so much fun to be had…

So what did I do for pretty much the first year I lived in Chicago? I sat on my ever-widening butt, that's what! Little Debbie and I were very close back then. Oh, can that woman bake a Swiss roll…but I digress.

I transferred with the company I was working for at the time. It was located in Burr Ridge and I was living on the North side of Chicago. While there were certainly social outlets with the people I worked with, the vast majority of them lived in the west and southwest suburbs. Not that those areas aren't lovely, but a suburb is a suburb is a suburb no matter where you are in America. AND heading out to Chicago's suburbs means a long commute to have a social life while defeating the purpose of living in the City.

About a year into living in Chicago, there I was, dating a nice girl from Naperville (met thru work of course) and she told me about a sports group in the City. I joined, and that was my salvation.

Over 12 years later, I'm still friends with the people I met during that first volleyball season. The group I joined wasn't run very well, but I liked the concept of getting people together to play sports and have social events so I started my own company, Sports Monster, which is now the largest of its kind in America.

Get A Life! In the City: Chicago, which provides information about Sports Monster, is an excellent guide for LIVING in Chicago. LIVING is the key word. Regardless of where you reside in America, it is important that you have the opportunity to get involved and take advantage of what's available for you to do so that you can do some living. What's more important is that you have the information so that you can make educated decisions about choosing what you can do to get your butt out of the house.

Too many people just sit in night after night and bemoan the fact that they don't have anything to do or friends to do things with. It definitely takes some gumption to get up the nerve to venture out to try something new by yourself. But you HAVE to make that move if you're ever going to meet new friends outside of your work environment and your other usual social circles.

Get A Life! In the City: Chicago provides newcomers to Chicago and natives alike, an array of ideas of what you can do to have fun. Sure, I would love it if you checked out what Sports Monster has to offer. One of Sports Monster's hallmarks is focusing on individuals. We create entirely new teams made up of individuals just like you to provide maximum bonding opportunities. However, not everyone (gasp!) is into sports. So why not try a ceramics class or volunteering at one of our local museums? The whole city awaits you to get involved and become an active Chicagoan.

I encourage you to read the entries provided in the guide, do additional research, ask your friends for their advice OR just take the plunge and see what happens. The worst that can happen is a wasted evening or afternoon, which will still make for a good story. The best that can happen is that you'll make a terrific bunch of new friends or discover something that you really enjoy.

Now where did I put those Little Debbie Oatmeal Cremes…?

Why It's Important to Get a Life! In the City

Several years ago, I thought I had discovered my true purpose in life - to become a high-powered marketing executive at a major international corporation in Europe. Boy, am I glad that life doesn't always give us what we think we want. To prepare myself for a profession in international business, I enrolled in an MBA program at a London university. The two years I spent living, studying, and working in London were tough. The workload was so heavy at times that I often felt life was nothing more than work and sleep.

My friends often told me that I had no life—hence the title for this book. After a challenging, yet successful, first semester, I took some time to examine my life and realized that something was missing. Actually, a lot was missing. My life had no balance. Not that I'm a big believer in astrology, but the symbol for my birth sign is a set of scales and my scales were completely out of whack. They were tipped in favor of work, work, and what else? More work. I made little time for friends, romantic relationships, a spiritual life and community involvement. Then, a sobering thought hit me. Wouldn't it be a tragedy if I came all the way to London—a place known for its diverse culture and activities—and didn't get out to experience it? At that moment, I decided to get a life in the city. But what did having a "life" really mean?

I looked up several definitions of the word and found that the following appeared in most of the definitions:

Animation
Existence *Vitality*
Energy *Spirit*
ENTHUSIASM

I then asked myself, "When was the last time I felt animated, energetic, enthusiastic, and full of vitality? What was I doing? Who was I with? Where was I?" I grabbed one of my notebooks and began writing down the answers. I felt the most animated was when I was debating with friends on a political or social issue dear to me. The times I felt the most energetic were after a really good workout or during a game of softball or volleyball. I had vitality and enthusiasm when I was discussing an idea for an entrepreneurial venture, visiting another country, or learning a foreign language. In all these situations, I was with friends or colleagues with whom I shared many of the same goals, values, and interests.

After this "ah ha" moment, I made a list of activities I enjoyed, the qualities I loved most about my closest friends and colleagues, and the things I've always wanted do. With this list in hand, I embarked upon a journey that turned out to be two of the best years of my life. I developed many close relationships. I made time for dating. I re-discovered my inner athlete by participating in sports. I continued to learn French, and even found new interests in healthy eating and holistic medicine.

Back to Chicago

I left London after I graduated and returned to Chicago to begin my dream job as a marketing executive for a major international corporation. I figured it would be easy to get acclimated to Chicago again since I had only been gone for two years. After all, I was born here, grew up here, and had many established friendships. Boy, was I wrong. Many of my friends had moved away, gotten married, started families, or were totally absorbed in their careers, which left me feeling disconnected. I then realized that I, too, was a different person with new interests. And in many ways, I was in a new city again. Immediately, I went through the same exercise I had gone through in London, and I'm glad to say that I've found balance right here at home in Chicago. Since I've returned from England, which has been 6 years now, I've done the LaSalle Chicago Marathon twice (I'm nuts right? :o); climbed the stairs of the John Hancock Building in an event called Hustle Up the Hancock twice; played volleyball with Sports Monster; took singing lessons; learned some improvisation techniques from a Second City Training Course; served as president of an investment club called the Multi-Millies; taught marketing at a Jr. College for two years; joined a few professional and social organizations and had lots of fun and made some good friends in the process.

Remember, no matter what city you find yourself in, do what you love. Find and unleash your passions, discover a new talent or interest, and above all, connect with a group of individuals—great relationships are what we cherish most in life. §

4-Steps to Getting a Life In the City!

When I lived in London and also when I came back to Chicago, I had to do a little soul searching to get a life. Everyone's soul searching experience will be unique, but I'm willing to bet each person's journey will include four main steps. There are so many activities to choose from in Chicago. Taking the following steps will help you to maximize your time and your life by doing the things that you are truly passionate about.

Get a Clue!
In the City!

Step 1: Get a Clue!
Re-discover Your Passions in Life

The first thing I'd encourage you to do is to search for and identify the things you want to experience here in the Windy City. A few questions you can ask yourself include:

Q. What did I enjoy as a kid that I would love to start doing again?

A. I used to be on the volleyball team in high school and I was really good. I really miss playing.

Q. What have I always wanted to do or experience that I just haven't made time for?

A. I've always wanted to learn ballet, but never had the opportunity to take lessons. It would be nice to learn now. Besides, It would be a great way to get in shape.

Q. What experiences or activities make me come alive?

A. There's something about theatre and being on stage that makes my soul sing. I really miss being able to perform in school plays.

Even if you enjoy the activities in your life or you have a good idea of what you love doing, it wouldn't hurt for you to take a moment and ask yourself these questions. You never know what new interests or talents may surface.

Get a Vision!
In the City!

Step 2: Get A Vision!
Envision the Life You Want in the Windy City

After you've gotten a clue and re-discovered your passions, imagine what your life would be like if you were to incorporate them into your lifestyle. For example, if you've always wanted to take acting or do stand-up comedy, imagine yourself with a group of fun and adventurous people having a great time learning some new skills. See yourself either becoming a comedian or simply making the crowd laugh during a speech you have to give at work. Imagine all of the people who will see a totally new side of you. Picture doors opening up for you as a result of this new skill or talent you've uncovered.

Get a Plan!
In the City!

Step 3: Get A Plan!
Create Your Very Own Get A Life! In the City Calendar

At this stage, you should feel like a kid who has just been set free in a playground. Now it's time to grab your favorite notebook and start making plans.

Make a list of what you want to do and then divide your list into the categories below. See the sample lists under each category for ideas:

- Take A Class! In the City
    - Learn to paint with watercolors, take some cooking classes, learn to belly dance
- Get Buff! In the City
    - Join a running group, train for a triathlon, go skiing, learn to sail, join a volleyball league
- Get Connected! In the City
    - Join a chamber of commerce, join a wine tasting group, join a dining club for singles
- Do Good! In the City
    - Serve the homeless, raise money for cancer awareness, help a child with homework
- Chill Out! In the City
    - Get a massage, take a walk in a garden, begin practicing yoga

Use this book to research some organizations that offer the activities you have chosen. Once you've gathered all of the information you need, pull out your calendar (or palm pilot) and schedule these activities into your life. If you plan to play volleyball with a league one night per week, plan for it. Block your calendar and take this time seriously. Unless there's an emergency, do not let anything prevent you from engaging in your chosen activity. Keeping these appointments with yourself is the only way to get and keep a life!

Step 4: Get A Life! In the City
It's Time for Action

Now, it's time to put your plan into action. You've envisioned yourself and how your life would be if you incorporated the things you enjoyed. You've made your plans and now it's time to implement them. Keep your list with you as a reminder of your desire to get and keep a life here in the Windy City. Put it in a place where you'll see it everyday. Remember, the only way to get a life in the City is if you incorporate what you love doing into your lifestyle.

This 4-step process has been a wonderful tool for me. It has truly helped me get and keep a life here in Chicago. I hope you have found it useful in having fun and experiencing a richer life.

I'd Love to Hear From You!

If Get A Life! In the City: Chicago has inspired you in some way or has given you some ideas on how you can get a life in and around the Windy City, please send me email. My email address is *sheena@getalifeinthecity.com*.

I'm also open to any suggestions. If there' is a category you'd like to see in future editions, please let me know.

For more information on things to do in the Chicago area, logon to *www.getalifeinthecity.com*. Learn more about interesting organizations in Chicago and learn how to get a customized Get A Life! In the City plan. §

Who Should Read this Book?

Newcomers

Returning Residents

Natives

Singles

Married

Couples

1. Newcomers

To those of you who are new to Chicago, welcome! The Windy City is one of the friendliest cities in the world. Chicagoans come from all walks of life and from just about every culture under the sun. If you want to know Chicago, get to know the people. We tend to be very active, so the more activities you participate in, the better you'll get to know both natives and non-natives alike. Use this book as a resource for deciding how you will get involved in Chicago life.

2. Returning Residents

To those who have returned to Chicago after living in another state or in my case another country, welcome to a new experience in this City you've called home for most of your life. You've probably visited the main attractions like the Museum of Science and Industry or the Shedd Aquarium about a million times and absolutely love these places. Chances are, you're ready to meet new people and become more involved in city life. Sometimes, when we've lived in a place all our lives, leave and then come back, we can both see and appreciate the people and the life enriching opportunities in our own back yard. I'd like to encourage you to explore Chicago like you explored the place you just returned from. Check out some of the organizations in this book. Develop your talents, discover new ones, build relationships, and just have a good time while you're home. Readjusting can be a bit difficult, especially when you first return, but hang in there. You'll soon be making the most out of life here in the Windy City.

3. Natives

Okay all you die-hard Chicagoans who've never left the City (or surrounding suburbs) for more than 3 weeks at a time, congratulations for picking up this book. The fact that you are open to learning more about what Chicago has to offer means that you're ready to expand your horizons. Use this guide as a resource for trying something new and for getting to know people you would not ordinarily meet in your usual social circles. You'll be amazed at how your life will be enhanced!

4. Busy Professionals

To all of you work-enthusiasts (I won't call you workaholics☺) who work more than 40 hours a week and spend very little time enjoying yourselves, congratulations for taking a stand. If your colleagues, family, and friends are telling you to "get a life!" take their advice. Turn off the pager and cell phone, and leave work at a decent hour to stretch your legs and do something fun. Use this book as a resource to help you incorporate other interests, hobbies, and plain old fun into your life again.

5. Singles

If you're single and lovin' it or single and looking to get hooked up, congratulations and welcome to an alternative strategy for meeting people, making friends, and dating. One of the keys to living the single life in Chicago is to take advantage of the numerous opportunities there are to have fun and to develop yourself. While you're out networking and pursuing hobbies or special interests, you're bound to make new friends or meet that someone special. This entire guidebook (not just the section on networking and socializing) will give you some ideas on how and where to meet and get to know people in the City.

6. Married Couples

To all the married couples who want to develop a talent or pursue a special interest either as individuals or as a couple, congratulations for being creative in keeping your marriage alive. Most of the activities highlighted in this guide can be done as individuals or as couples. Many happily married couples tell me that the key to their success is balancing their needs as a couple with their needs as individuals. I encourage you to use this guide as a resource for pursuing your interests.

Good luck and have fun while you *Get A Life! In the City.*

Language

Take a Class!

Art

Dance

Music

Personal Growth

Acting

Cooking

Writing

Acting

Language

Social Science

Philosophy

Take a Class!

www.getalifeinthecity.com

Take A Class! In the City

Have you always wanted to learn to paint, act, cook, dance, or speak a foreign language just for the thrill of it? If the answer is yes, you're in the perfect city. Not only is Chicago home to some of the nation's top schools, it is also home to organizations that give the average person like you and me the opportunity to learn something new. About a year ago, I took an improv class and absolutely loved it. I'm no Whoopi Goldberg or the female version of Wayne Brady—at least not yet, but I've learned some very creative ways to break the ice or ease tension during meetings at work. A friend of mine that I met while in the class completed the entire improv series. She went on to star in an independent film which ran at a suburban AMC theatre for several weeks. See what hidden talents can emerge and develop while taking a class?

In addition to taking classes for fun, I've also taken classes to either further my career or to learn about a field or an industry that I find exciting. Several years ago, I took a class in restaurant management because I had been thinking about buying a franchise. I was excited about the prospect of owning a restaurant, but felt I needed to be grounded in the reality of managing and operating a restaurant before actually making the purchase. Taking this class was one of the best decisions I've made. By the end of the semester, I realized that restaurant ownership was a very tough job requiring long hours. I also realized that the risks were high because many restaurants go out of business within 3 months. After considering the not so glamorous aspects of restaurant ownership, I decided not to become a restaurant owner. This class helped me to avoid a serious career and investment mistake.

The following section lists classes that are available in a wide variety of categories, in the City and suburbs. Many of these classes are recreational, but you never know where they may take you.

Arts, Crafts, and More
in the City!

artScape Chicago

66 E. Randolph St.
Chicago, IL 60601
Ph. 312-744-8925/ Fax 312-744-9249
www.Gallery37.org/artScape

Discover your creativity at artScape Chicago, an art program run through Harold Washington College. Most classes offered by artScape Chicago are held at the Gallery 37 Center for the Arts. This organization features computer art classes for adults, which include Beginning Video Art, Digital Imaging, and Web Page Design. This program also offers more traditional art classes like Beginning Drawing and Painting, Calligraphy, Drawing with Pastels, and Ceramics. Other classes include Foreign Languages, Dance (such as Belly and African dancing), Music, Photography, and Yoga.

Bauhaus Apprenticeship Institute

6525 N. Clark St.
Chicago, IL 60626
Ph.773-338-1746
http://lf.org/bhai2000/

Do you have fond memories of your high school shop class? Well, the Bauhaus Apprenticeship Institute, which specializes in training its students in the art of furniture making, may be right up your alley. The Institute offers community education classes for beginning as well as advanced woodworking students. Advanced students can apply for a full-time apprenticeship-training program to further enhance their skills.

Cole Studio

410 S. Michigan Ave., Suite 306
Chicago, IL 60605
Ph. 312-362-9890
www.gracecole.com

The Cole Studio, led by artist Grace Cole, offers classes in drawing
and oil painting that encourage students to discover themselves
through the artistic process. Students who are serious about learning
to draw or oil paint will receive individualized attention because class
sizes are limited to only five students at a time. The Cole Studio serves
beginning to advanced students willing to explore. Cole also offers
special workshops such as The Creativity Workshop, which is held in
France's Loire Valley for two weeks.

The Drawing Workshop

4410 N. Ravenswood Ave.
Chicago, IL 60613
Ph. 773-728-1127

If you like to draw or want to learn how, then this place may be right
for you. The Drawing Workshop offers classes in Basic Drawing,
Figure Drawing, and Skeletal Sculpturing with Clay. Open Figure
Drawing workshops are also offered and held on Sundays.

DuPage Art League

218 W. Front St.
Wheaton, IL 60187
Ph. 630-653-7090
www.dupageartleague.org

Get in touch with your inner artist at the DuPage Art League. This non-profit school and gallery offers affordable art classes such as Basic and Advanced Figure Drawing, Oil and Acrylic Painting, Traditional Watercolor, Photography, Anatomy, Pastels, Paper and Clay Sculpture, Printmaking, Papermaking, Collage and Mixed Media, Botanical Painting, Cartooning and Animation and more. Classes are typically scheduled in three-week sessions. Workshops, demonstrations, and exhibits are held regularly. "Paint-Outs" or group painting activities are also held at various outdoor locations.

Ed Hinkley Watercolor Classes & Workshops

4052 N. Western Ave.
Chicago, IL 60618
Ph. 773-539-6047

If you have an interest in watercolor painting, try the Ed Hinkley Studio. Classes are composed of beginners with no previous experience and more advanced students looking to further develop their skills. Beginners will develop an understanding of watercolor painting by practicing and experimenting with a variety of brushes, papers and mediums. Advanced students will further develop their own unique style as well as explore exhibition opportunities. Class sizes are small with a minimum of three and a maximum of six students. Private and group lessons are also available.

Evanston Art Center

2603 Sheridan Rd.
Evanston, IL 60201
Ph. 847-475-5300/Fax 847-475-5330
www.evanstonartcenter.org

The Evanston Art Center (EAC) is one of the oldest and largest visual arts centers in the state. EAC is the perfect place for the beginner or professional artist because of its wide variety of art classes for adults and children. There are over 100 classes and workshops in Photography, Ceramics, Painting, Sculpting, Jewelry Making and more. Class sizes are small, the studios are very well-equipped, the faculty is impressive, and the lakeside setting is beautiful.

Fire Arts Center of Chicago

1800 W. Cuyler
Chicago, IL 60613
Ph. 773-271-7710
www.firearts.org

If you've ever been curious about sculpting or furniture making, then stop by the Fire Arts Center of Chicago (FAC). FAC is a non-profit organization that promotes fire arts—the art of creating objects like metal furniture and sculpture. Classes at FAC include Basic and Advanced Metal Sculpture, Metal Furniture Making, Bronze and Iron Metal Casting, Basic and Advanced Moldmaking, Forging, Figure Sculpture, and much more. For current students and alumni alike, FAC also offers open studio time.

Park West Ceramics

719 W. Wrightwood
Chicago, IL 60614
Ph. 773-296-2160
www.parkwestceramics.com

Park West Ceramics is a great place to explore your passion to play with clay. This organization offers classes for beginners as well as advanced ceramics students. Wheelthrowing and Handbuilding classes are offered in eight-week sessions, and meet once a week for about three hours. This organization prides itself on providing a fun and constructive environment for its students. Open studio time is also available.

Glass Frog Studio

775 W. Jackson Blvd., 5th Floor
Chicago, IL 60661
Ph. 773-454-3456/Fax 312-733-0072
www.glassfrogstudio.com

The Glass Frog Studio is an independent art studio located in Greek Town that offers ceramics classes for beginning to intermediate students. Class sizes are small so that each student receives individual attention. Students learn Handbuilding and Wheelthrowing, Cup, Bowl, and Cylinder Construction, and much more. Class sessions usually last for eight weeks and enrollment is continuous. This place is ideal for people with busy schedules or who travel a lot because the studio allows students to make up classes.

Hyde Park Art Center

5307 S. Hyde Park Blvd.
Chicago, IL 60615
Ph. 773-324-5520/Fax 773-324-6641
www.hydeparkart.org

The Hyde Park Art Center (HPAC) has been around for over 60 years. HPAC has served residents of the Kenwood and Hyde Park communities by offering classes in Photography, Drawing, Oil Painting, Calligraphy, Multi-media, Jewelry Making, and Fiber Arts. It also offers a community outreach program that brings arts and crafts to many children and adults living throughout the City.

La Grange Art League

122 Calendar Ct.
La Grange, IL 60525
Ph. 708-352-1480
www.lagrangeartleague.org

The La Grange Art League offers classes in drawing and painting in the Western suburbs. Classes include Beginning and Intermediate Watercolor, Basic Drawing and Sketching, Creative Drawing and Painting, Pastels, Oils, Silk Painting, and more.

Lill Street Art Center

4401 N. Ravenswood
Chicago, IL 60640
Ph. 773-769-4226
www.lillstreet.com

Ever had an interest or a knack for pottery or jewelry making? In addition to the traditional drawing and painting classes, this art center offers classes and workshops for adults and children in ceramics, sculpture, jewelry making/metalsmithing, and multi-media art. The Lill Street Art Center contains several classrooms and holds over 150 classes and workshops each session. Classes are taught by professional artists and include Beginning and Intermediate Drawing, Beginning and Intermediate Oil Painting, Acrylic Painting, Watercolor, Vietnamese Silk Painting, and more. This art center is also one of the Midwest's largest ceramic centers and is open to the public all year round. Generous open studio time is also available.

Northshore Art League

620 Lincoln Ave.
Winnetka, IL 60093
Ph. 847-446-2870
www.northshoreartleague.org

The North Shore Art League has been around for over 76 years. Located in the Northern suburbs, this art league offers unique art classes for adults and children at very reasonable prices. Class titles have included Drawing and Painting, Decorative Art in Clay, Cartooning, Art in the Gardens, Summer Watercolor Nights, Outdoor Watercolor, and Creative Figure Studio. Special workshops and panel discussions are also held on topics like how an artist should prepare his or her work for group shows.

Oak Park Art League

720 Chicago Ave.
Oak Park, IL 60302
Ph. 708-386-9853/Fax 708-386-4893
www.opal-art.com

The Oak Park Art League has been around for over 80 years providing art instruction to the surrounding community. Beginners, as well as advanced art students, can enhance their skills while having lots of fun in the process. Classes and workshops offered include Watercolor, Drawing and Painting, Oil Painting, Collage, and Clay. Other popular classes include Knitting, Meditation, and Yoga.

Old Town Art Center

1763 N. North Park Ave.
Chicago, IL 60614
Ph. 312-337-1938/Fax 312-337-4015
www.oldtowntriangle.com

The Old Town Arts Center takes a "holistic" approach to arts and crafts by encouraging its students to discover their inner artist. Both professional and non-professional artists come to take advantage of classes like Figure Drawing and Painting, Watercolor, Oil Painting, and Life Drawing. Artists can also relax and tap into the creativity within by taking Yoga classes.

Ox-Bow

37 S. Wabash
Chicago, IL 60603
Ph. 1-800-318-3019
www.ox-bow.org

Located in beautiful Saugatuck, Michigan, Ox-Bow is a summer art school as well as a residency for artists. It's affiliation with the Art Institute of Chicago and its distance from the City makes Ox-Bow the perfect place for both novice and professional artists who are looking for a creative summer get away. Both credit and non-credit courses are offered for one to two-week intervals between the months of June and August. Classes offered include Painting, Drawing, Print Making, Ceramics, Metals, Performance, Paper Making, Creative Writing, Glass Blowing, Foundry, and Sculpture. The beautiful beaches, trees, and sand dunes provide the perfect setting in which to be inspired.

Palette & Chisel Academy of Fine Arts

1012 N. Dearborn Pkwy.
Chicago, IL 60610
Ph. 312-642-4400/Fax 312-642-4317
www.paletteandchisel.org

The Palette & Chisel Academy has specialized in developing and motivating artists for over 105 years. Classes are offered in Life Drawing, Oil Painting, Sculpture, Watercolor, Art Anatomy, Chinese Brush Painting, and more. 50 hours of open studio sessions are also offered on a weekly basis with live models.

Riverside Arts Center

32 E. Quincy St.
Riverside, IL 60546
Ph. 708-442-6400
www.riversideartscenter.com

This organization began as an informal group that was committed to fostering a nurturing environment for those dedicated to the arts. The Riverside Art Center offers Arts & Crafts classes for both adults and children all year round. Classes for adults include Painting, Ceramics, and Gardening. Creative Writing classes are also available.

Suburban Fine Arts Center

1957 Sheridan Rd.
Highland Park, IL 60035
Ph. 847-432-1888/Fax 847-432-9106
www.sfac.net

The Suburban Fine Arts Center (SFAC) has been around for 43 years. Located in the Northern suburbs, SFAC offers classes and workshops for adults and children in Painting, Drawing, Photography, Ceramics, Jewelry Making, Collage, Silk Painting, Knitting, Sculpting, Mosaics, and Botanical Drawing. If you've ever wondered how to design a greeting card, make a dreamcatcher, or arrange flowers like a professional, this is a great place to get started because there are workshops to show you how. Classes and workshops are offered all year round, during the day, at night and on the weekends.

Terra Incognito Studios & Gallery

246 Chicago Ave.
Oak Park, IL 60302
Ph. 708-383-6228
www.terraincognitostudios.com

In case you're wondering, the name Terra Incognito means, "earth in disguise." This Oak Park art studio and gallery offers classes for both adults and children in Ceramics including Wheelthrowing and Handbuilding. The studio also offers open studio time.

The School of the Art Institute of Chicago

37 S. Wabash Ave.
Chicago, IL 60603
Ph. 312-899-5100
www.artic.edu

If you wish to take your passion for art to the next level, the Art Institute of Chicago is the place to take both credit and non-credit art classes. The Art Institute attracts a diverse and intelligent student body and faculty, and fosters the development of creativity. Classes and workshops offered here include Drawing, Painting, Printmaking, Sculpture, Ceramics, Photography, Fashion & Fiber, Illustration and Graphic Design.

TLD Design Center & Gallery

26 E. Quincy St.
Westmont, IL 60559
Ph. 630-963-9573
www.tlddesigns.com

TLD Design Center & Gallery offers a wide variety of classes in the Western suburbs. Classes include Drawing, Collage & Paper Art, Crochet & Knitting, Felt Making & Spinning, Glass Bead Making, Jewelry Design, Pottery, Textile Design, Weaving, Hat Making, Soap Making, and Candle Making. There are classes for adults and children.

Triangle Camera, Inc.

3445 N. Broadway
Chicago, IL 60657
Ph. 773-472-1015
www.trianglecamera.com

This is a great place to hone your photography skills if you have a passion for pictures. Triangle Camera is a family owned, full-service neighborhood camera store that includes a school of photography. Classes offered here include Basic Photography, Intermediate Photography, Black and White Photography, Darkroom, Digital Introduction, and Portrait Studio.

Vital Projects, Ltd.

1579 N. Milwaukee Ave., Suite 230
Chicago, IL 60622
Ph. 773-489-0455/Fax 773-489-0481
www.vitalprojects.com

Vital Projects offers instruction to individuals who want to learn photography techniques as well as gain a better understanding of the creative process. Vital Projects has facilities that include a darkroom and studio. This organization offers a wide variety of classes and workshops such as Camera Function and Technique, Basic Darkroom Techniques, Advanced Darkroom Workshop, Impact Lighting, Color Photography, View Camera (Basics of operating 4x5 view), Creative Photography Series, Headshots, Pinhole Photography, Digital Camera, and more. Class sizes are between four and ten students. For students interested in pursuing photography seriously, a residency program is offered.

J. Miller Handcrafted Furniture

1774 W. Lunt Ave.
Chicago, IL 60626
Ph. 773-761-3311/Fax 773-761-7546
www.furnituremaking.com

J. Miller Handcrafted Furniture, run by craftsman Jeff Miller, offers classes and workshops covering three categories—furniture making, skill workshops, and master classes. Specific classes and workshops include Table Making, Chair Making, Woodworking Skills, Dovetail Workshop, Mortise and Tenon, Making and Using Jigs, Shaping and Bending Curves, Hand Tools Workshops, Router Master, and Table Saw Master. An apprenticeship program is also available to those seriously committed to furniture making.

Gallery 37

66 E. Randolph St.
Chicago, IL 60601
Ph. 312-744-8925/Fax 312-744-9249
www.Gallery37.org/adult/artscape

Gallery 37 is a non-profit organization dedicated to creating mentoring relationships between professional artists and Chicago's youth. Aspiring young artists are given not only the opportunity to work with professional artists, but also the chance to earn a living. Every year, young people between the ages of 14-21, regardless of their economic background, race, or gender, work as apprentice artists in areas such as Mural Painting, Poetry, African Dance, Web site Design or Theatre. There is also a pre-employment program available for children ages 10 to 13. There are several ways to get involved with Gallery 37. If you're an artist and want to give back to the community, you can become a mentor in this program. Other volunteer opportunities include classroom and field trip assistants, resume and interview tutors, and program ambassadors at special events and festivals.

Archeworks

625 N. Kingsbury St.
Chicago, IL 60610
Ph. 312-867-7254/Fax 312-867-7260
www.archeworks.org

Is the design or architecture of a building or landmark intriguing to you? Do you have some architecture or design expertise and want to sharpen your skills? If the answer is yes to either of these questions, then check out Archeworks. Founded in 1994, Archeworks is a non-profit organization dedicated to serving the surrounding community while helping to increase the knowledge and experience of its design and architecture students.

Students accepted into this unique, multi-disciplinary design school will have the opportunity to make a difference by developing design and architecture solutions to benefit people who may be physically challenged, elderly, living with AIDS, or living in poverty. Applicants from educational and professional backgrounds outside of design and architecture are considered.

Acting, Theatre and Film in the City!

Act One Studios

640 N. LaSalle St., Suite. 535
Chicago, IL 60610
Ph. 312-787-9384
www.actone.com

The Act One Studios challenges you to "amaze your friends and horrify your parents" by taking the acting plunge. Anyone serious about acting should take a class here. This acting school, which offers classes for beginning to advanced students, is pretty intense, but classes are lots of fun. Classes and workshops include Commercial Technique, Commercial Acting, TV & Film, Audition Techniques, Industrial Film/Ear Prompter, Voice & Speech, Radio & Television Voice Acting, Stand-up Comedy, and Yoga for Actors. This is a great place to take classes even if your goal is only to improve your communication skills.

Chicago Center for Performing Arts

777 N. Green St.
Chicago, IL 60622
Ph. 312-327-2040
www.theaterland.com

The Chicago Center for the Performing Arts (CCPA) offers a wide variety of classes in performing arts. Departments at the CCPA include The Chicago Training Center (CTC), the School of Music, The Player's Workshop, and the Writing Program. The CTC offers acting classes like Acting Technique, On Camera Technique, Musical Theatre, and Plastiscene—physical theatre, physical listening, and physical creativity. Beginning and intermediate improv training as well as corporate improv workshops are offered through The Player's Workshop, which is the country's oldest school of improv. The School of Music offers classes and private instruction. Private lessons are offered in Flute, Violin, Percussion, Double Bass, Saxophone, Piano, Voice, and Guitar. There are also classes in jazz improvisation and small jazz ensemble.

Chicago Dramatists

1105 W. Chicago Ave.
Chicago, IL 60622
Ph. 312-633-0630
www.chicagodramatists.org

Since 1979, the Chicago Dramatists organization has been in the business of developing playwrights. Not only does this theatre promote the works of new playwrights, it also offers instruction. Types of classes offered include Developing a Play, Dialogue Workshop, Playwriting, and Screenwriting.

Comedy College

2951 N. Greenview
Chicago, IL 60657
Ph. 773-250-7979
www.comedycollegeinfo.com

The Comedy College helps anyone interested in developing his or her sense of humor. Classes offered include Stand-up Comedy 101, Comedy College Improv, and Sketchwriting. Students will learn how to write, edit and deliver their own work. Graduation from the classes is a live performance with friends and family in the audience. This is a great way to inject humor into your life, improve your communication skills, and build self-confidence.

Comedy Sportz

2851 N. Halsted St.
Chicago, IL 60657
Ph. 773-549-8080 ext. 224/Fax 773-549-8142
www.comedysportzchicago.com

Housed in a newly renovated theatre in Chicago's Lakeview area, Comedy Sportz is the place to go to learn the short-form style of improv. Comedy Sportz University offers four levels of classes including The Fundamentals of Improv (101); Intermediate Improv (202); The Comedy Sportz Games (303); and The Performance Level (404). This series of classes takes students from beginning improvisers—focusing on elements such as active listening and spontaneity—to more mature improvisers developing scene work and the ability to work synergistically with other improv characters. Each class ends with a graduation where students perform in front of a live audience consisting of their family and friends.

The Actor's Gymnasium

927 Noyes St.
Evanston, IL 60201
Ph. 847-328-2795/Fax 847-328-3495
www.actorsgymnasium.com

If you've ever dreamed of being part of Circ du Soleil or wondered what it was like to engage in stage fights, you should take a closer look at The Actor's Gymnasium. The Actor's Gymnasium and Performing Arts School offers training in physical performing arts such as Circus Arts. Circus Arts include Juggling, Stilt-Walking, Tightrope Walking, Trapeze, Clowning, Gymnastics, Stage Combat, and much more. This type of theatre training will allow you to get in touch with your body by combining physical movement with imagination and creativity.

The Audition Studio

20 W. Hubbard, Suite 2E
Chicago, IL 60610
Ph. 312-527-4566
www.theauditionstudio.com

Are you waiting to be discovered? Well check out the Audition Studio, an organization that has been training actors and actresses in Chicago for over 20 years. Classes offered include Intro to Shurtleff I & II, Improv for Actors, Scene & Study, Advanced Scene & Study, Cold Reading, Master Audition Class, Audition Technique for Theatre, Monologue Workshops, On Camera, Beginning & Intermediate Voiceover, and Beginning Acting.

The Second City Training Center

1616 N. Wells St.
Chicago, IL 60614
Ph. 312-664-3959/Fax 312-664-9837
www.secondcity.com

Have you ever wanted to be quick on your feet and funny like Wayne Brady and Drew Carey on the hit TV show "Who's Line is it Anyway?" Or better yet, are you looking for a fun and "quirky" way to relax, have a little fun, and be more at ease around people? If you answered "yes" to either of these questions, improv at The Second City Training Center may be the thing for you. This world-renowned school holds classes and workshops all year round, in Improvisation, Acting, and Comedy Writing for beginning to advanced students. And since many companies are seeing the value of improv skills in business, corporate classes are also offered. Whether your goal is to break into the entertainment industry or to simply have some fun, chances are The Second City Training Center has something for you.

Barbizon

1051 Perimeter Dr. Suite 950
Schaumburg, IL 60173
Ph. 847-240-4200/Fax 847-413-2099
www.modelsmidwest.com

Barbizon's motto, "Train to be a Model, or Just Look Like One", reflects what it has to offer. This is a great place for anyone wanting to polish his or her look and have fun in the process. Whether your goal is to make it in the modeling industry or to boost your self-confidence, Barbizon has a class you'll enjoy. This modeling school mainly caters to the young, but if you're young at heart, you'll get the most out of your experience. Topics of instruction include Runway Modeling, Hair and Make-up, Fashion, On-Camera Acting Techniques, Successful Photo Shoots, and much more.

Voice Power/Helen Cutting

445 E. Ohio St., Suite 1914
Chicago, IL 60611
Ph. 312-527-1809
www.voicepowr.com

Voice Power, run by accomplished voice coach Helen Cutting, offers customized vocal training for individuals as well as groups. Helen's courses and methods deliver very noticeable results, often in a very short period of time. Types of vocal training include Voice and Speech Improvement, Public Speaking, Accent Reduction, Voice Over, Media Training, and Communication Skills. Helen prepares a customized program with your vocal goals and needs in mind. She also gives you tapes from your coaching sessions so you can practice the vocal exercises at home and track your improvement over the length of the course.

Piven Theatre Workshop

927 Noyes St.
Evanston, IL 60201
Ph. 847-866-6597
www.piventheatre.org

The Piven Theatre Workshop offers a variety of classes, including Piven 101 where students play theatre games, learn improv, and study scenes, movement, and story theatre. An advanced class in monologue is also offered. Students of the Piven Theatre Workshop come for a variety of reasons, including personal enrichment and the development of professional acting skills.

Community Film Workshop of Chicago

1130 South Wabash, Suite 302
Chicago, IL 60605
Ph. 312-427-1245/Fax 312-427-8818
www.cfwchicago.or

Community Film Workshop of Chicago (CFWC) has been providing film and video education for over 30 years. CFWC is a media access center that offers classes for the novice as well as the more advanced video and film student. The types of classes offered include Beginning and Advanced Digital Video Production, Video Editing, Film History and Aesthetics, and more.

Chicago Filmmakers

5243 N. Clark St., 2nd Floor
Chicago, IL 60640
Ph. 773-293-1447/Fax 773-293-0575
www.chicagofilmmakers.org

Whether you'd like to become the next Stephen Spielberg or to simply know firsthand how films are made, Chicago Filmmakers should be on your list of film schools to check out. Chicago Filmmakers is an independent film school that's been around for over 30 years. This school promotes an appreciation and an understanding of film and video as an art form as well as a means of self-expression. Chicago Filmmakers is very active in the community, offering access and opportunities to media to diverse audiences. Classes offered include Film Production I & II, Video I, Directing, Screenwriting, Documentary, and more. They also offer workshops and seminars on topics such as Camera Operation, Low-Budget Lighting, and DVD Authoring.

Chicago Access Network (CAN TV)

322 S. Green St., Suite 100
Chicago, IL 60607
Ph. 312-738-1400/Fax 312-738-2519
www.cantv.org

Chicago Access Network (CAN TV) offers free sessions on the low-cost opportunities of media/video production to individuals who are residents of Chicago. This television network provides a forum for Chicagoans to discuss local issues, promote educational and economic resources available to the community, and promote local talent and special initiatives. CAN TV is 90% local and non-commercial. In order to take advantage of these free sessions, you must be a City of Chicago resident. Contact CAN TV for more details.

The Screenwriters Group

1803 W. Byron
Chicago, IL 60613
Ph. 773-665-8500/Fax 773-665-9475
www.screenwritersgroup.com

If you've ever had an idea for a movie, this is an organization worth looking into. Classes held in Chicago have included How to Turn your Movie Idea into a Screenplay, How to Sell Your Screenplay and Creating Great Characters. This organization also offers an all day workshop entitled "The Obstacle Course" that puts your idea to the test. Instructors are positioned at various stations, which represent the development stages of a screenplay. Students rotate around each stage of development, getting feedback about the marketability of their movie ideas. For the more serious screenwriter, there are also longer-term courses available that can last up to two years.

Cooking
in the City!

The American Institute of Wine & Food
Chicago Chapter

Ph. 312-440-9290

The Chicago chapter of the American Institute of Wine & Food (AIWF) offers a variety of educational opportunities for enjoying wine and food. AIWF Chicago sponsors many events including wine tastings, food and wine pairings, cooking seminars and demonstrations, dining tours, and regular social gatherings.

Calphalon Culinary Center

1000 W. Washington St.
Chicago, IL 60607
Ph. 312-529-0100/Fax 866-623-2089
www.calphaonculinarycenter.com

The Calphalon Culinary Center is a modern cooking facility designed for cooks of all levels. The 8,000 square-foot center houses a lecture hall that seats 60 people, a classroom with 12 individual workstations, and a commercial kitchen. There is also a beautifully decorated dining area and wine cellar on the premises. Hands-on cooking classes include Knife Skills, Pasta, Mexican, Pork 101, Cake Decorating, Beef 101, Couples Cooking, Chicken 101, Breakfast, Soups, Cookies, and Creole. Private, customized classes and team building events are also offered. Other activities include guest chef demonstrations, lectures, cooking tours, and wine tasting.

Take A Class! In the City

Coachouse Gourmet

Ph. 847-724-1521
www.coachousegourmet.com

Julie Kearney founded the Coachouse Gourmet Cooking School in
1991. Classes, which are taught in her home in the Northwest suburbs,
have included the 30 Minute Gourmet (where 6 entrees are prepared
in 30 minutes or less), Fall Dinner, Pantry and Freezer Cooking, Fall
Soups, Quick Breads, Appetizers, and more.

Cook From Scratch

PO Box 543877
Chicago, IL 60654
Ph. 312-559-0052/Fax 312-655-0767
www.cookfromscratch.com

Chef Bridget Weis, owner of Cook From Scratch, offers a wide variety
of cooking classes such as Knife Skills, Cake Decorating, Baking
Basics, and Cooking Basics. She allows students to create their own
classes and workshops to focus on a particular skill or to simply try
out a recipe with a little help. Team building events and parties are
also available for bridal showers, gourmet clubs, and other groups.
Cook From Scratch classes are a great way to connect and have fun
with friends and colleagues.

Cooking with Best Chefs

1N446 Goodrich Ave.
Glen Ellyn, IL 60137
Ph. 630-793-0600/Fax 630-793-0288
www.BestChefs.com

Founded almost a decade ago by Bill Lavery, Cooking with Best
Chefs is one of the most unique membership organizations for those

interested in food and cooking. Classes led by well-known chefs, have been held throughout the Chicagoland area at popular department stores, hotels, and restaurants, and include ethnic cooking such as Cajun, Mediterranean, Italian, and Greek. Seasonal cooking classes include Thanksgiving and Christmas specialties. Cooking with Best Chefs also offers local, national, and international cooking trips, local restaurant tours, and wine dinners.

Chefs On Call

Chicago, IL 60614
Ph. 312-787-9451
www.chefsoncall.com

Owned by Chef Mark Costello, alumnus of the Culinary Institute of America in New York, Chefs on Call offers a number of customized cooking classes right in the privacy of your own home. Menus are based on whatever you or your group are interested in learning to cook. Contact Chefs on Call for further details on specific menus and classes.

Chez Madelaine School of Cooking & Cooking Tours

Ph. 630-655-0355
www.chezm.com

Madelaine of Chez Madelaine Cooking School has been teaching students the skills of cooking and baking since the late 1970's. Class and workshop topics have included Soups, Game, Baking, and Meals for Special Occasions. In addition to local classes, students can take advantage of international cooking tours. A group of students goes to France to learn about the country, the culture, and the cuisine. Madelaine also teaches cooking classes at the Alliance Française de Chicago (see page 39).

ChicaGourmets

www.chicagourmets.com
Ph. 708-383-7543/Fax 708-383-4964

Since 1997, ChicaGourmets (Chicago Gourmets) has been educating its members about food and fine dining in fun and creative ways. Members enjoy visiting trendy restaurants, staying current with what's going on in the food world, and meeting renowned food and wine experts. Wine tastings, special luncheons, private tours, cooking demonstrations, and book signings are among the many member activities planned throughout the year. Members also enjoy discounted events and a monthly newsletter.

Uncorked Chicago

www.uncorkedchicago.com

If you enjoy meeting new people and love wine, or want to learn more about wine, Uncorked Chicago is a great organization worth looking into. Membership is free, and you are sent emails of the wine tasting and wine related events. Also, on the website, there is a wine glossary and other information about wine.

Chopping Block Cooking School

1324 W. Webster Ave.
Chicago, IL 60614
Ph. 773-472-6700
www.thechoppingblock.net

Located in Lincoln Park, the Chopping Block School offers a wide variety of cooking classes for everyday cooks. Classes are offered throughout the year in Ethnic, Vegetarian, and Seasonal Cooking. Other classes include Wine Tasting, Knife Skills, and Entertaining.

Classes are taught by professional chefs and are small in size with a limit of 16 students.

Culinary Historians of Chicago

2113 Sanborn Circle
Plainfield, IL 60544
Ph. 815-439-3960
www.culinaryhistorians.org

Founded in 1993, The Culinary Historians of Chicago is an organization dedicated to educating people in the cultural history of food and drink. This non-profit organization meets monthly and sponsors lecture series and food and wine tours locally, nationally, and internationally.

French Culinary Experience

281 Messner Dr.
Wheeling, IL 60090
Ph. 847-215-1931
www.frenchcookingschool.com

Founded in 1988 by chefs Michel Coatrieux and Patrick Chabert, the French Cooking School teaches top-notch cooking techniques in French cuisine. The school has two kitchens—one used for demonstrations and another used for hands on experience. This organization offers classes such as Stocks & Sauces, Pates & Terrines, Basics of Cooking, Fish & Shellfish, Chocolate, Knife Handling, Vegetables & Soups, Beef Wellington, and Gingerbread House. Students have an opportunity to watch a meal being prepared as well as interact with the chefs. The school also offers private cooking lessons and in-home presentations. If you like to combine eating with traveling, the French Cooking School frequently arranges cooking tours to France.

Sur La Table Culinary Center

52-54 E. Walton St.
Chicago, IL 60611
Ph. 312-337-0600/Fax 312-337-7454
www.surlatable.com

Sur La Table offers the finest cooking equipment and accessories. This upscale cooking store began in Seattle's Pike's Peak Market and has spread to the Midwest. Sur La Table in Chicago complements its selection of fine cookery with a comprehensive culinary program, which offers a cooking class on just about every day of the week. The culinary program includes Cooking Fundamentals, The Glorious Foods of Greece, Basic Knife Skills, Single Guy Cooking, Single Gal Cooking, Baking Basics, Sushi for Beginners, Wok Cooking Made Easy, Cake Decorating, Italian Basics and much, much more. Classes are also available at the Naperville location.

Whole Foods

www.wholefoods.com

Whole Foods Market, the world's largest retailer of natural and organic foods, offers a variety of cooking classes, demonstrations, and seminars on healthy eating and better living. Classes vary by location and season and have included Vegetarian Cooking, Sushi Making, and French Bistro. Other healthy living classes and events held at some store locations include Active Meditation and Stress Management. Some stores even offer educational tours for groups interested in healthy lifestyles. Check out the web site for a location near you.

Williams & Sonoma

900 N. Michigan Ave.
Chicago, IL 60611
Ph. 312-587-8080

Williams and Sonoma is an upscale cooking equipment and supply store that offers cooking classes at many of its locations. Classes usually take place in the evenings and can vary by season and location. Some classes have featured Desserts, Cooking With Spices, Seafood, Cooking With Herbs, Spanish Desserts, Vegetarian, and more.

World Kitchen

66 E. Randolph St.
Chicago, IL 60601
Ph. 312-742-8497 or 312-744-8925/Fax 312-744-9249
www.worldkitchenchicago.org

World Kitchen, part of Gallery 37, offers cooking classes like Fall Fiesta, Chinese New Year, Christmas Traditions, and Late Harvest. Classes at World Kitchen tend to sell out quickly so try to get tickets shortly after a new schedule is published. Classes are very affordable, and are taught by some of Chicago's finest chefs.

International Kitchen

330 N. Wabash, Suite 3005
Chicago, IL 60611
Ph. 312-726-4525 or 800-945-8606
www.theinternationalkitchen.com

The International Kitchen effectively combines cooking and travel. Founded by Karen Kerbst in 1994, the organization plans cooking tours to France and Italy that range from four to eleven nights, depending on the tour. Past cooking tours include Bordeaux Cuisine at Chateau des Vigiers, Rhode School of Cuisine Le Mas Des Oliviers, Cooking en Provence, Cooking Class in Paris, Walking and Cooking in Tuscany, and Biking and Cooking in Tuscany.

Italidea

500 N. Michigan Ave., Suite 1450
Chicago, IL 60611
Ph. 312-832-9545/Fax 312-822-9622
www.iicch.org

Italidea offers two eight-week cooking courses that combine learning to cook Italian food with learning to speak Italian. Classes are either held at a popular Chicago Italian restaurant or at the home of a faculty member. Italidea also offers a six-week wine class that teaches students about Italian wines.

Rustic Kitchen

723 West Brompton Ave., Suite 2W
Chicago, IL 60657
Ph. 773-935-4239
www.rustickitchen.com

Janine MacLachlan, founder of the Rustic Kitchen, teaches cooking classes in her Chicago home. Past classes have included Mediterranean, French, Breakfast Foods, Finger Foods, Mixed Grill, and more.

College of DuPage County

425 Fawell Blvd.
Glen Ellyn, IL 60127
Ph. 630-942-2208 or 630-942-2800
www.cod.edu/conted

The Culinary and Home Program at the College of DuPage offers non-credit courses in cooking that feature local cookbook authors as well as executive chefs. Both single-session and multi-session cooking classes are available. Class categories include nutritional cooking and wine tasting. There are also multi-course food and wine dinners held at some of the areas finest restaurants.

Kendall College

2408 Orrington Ave.
Evanston, IL 60201
Ph. 847-448-2550
www.kendall.edu

Kendall College's School of Culinary Arts offers a program for non-professional cooks of all levels through its Spice Up Your Life program. Most classes are offered on Saturdays, but a few classes are offered in the evenings during the week. Classes are taught by professional chef instructors and include Basic and Advanced Knife Skills, Breads, Ethnic Cuisines, Appetizers, Soups and Stews, Cooking with Beer, Candy Making, and more.

Elgin Community College

1700 Spartan Dr.
Elgin, IL 60123
Ph. 847-622-3036
www.elgin.edu

Elgin Community College offers a wide variety of non-credit cooking classes including Gourmet Cooking, Desserts and Pastries, and Ethnic Cuisine. Students can learn to create Indian Curry Dishes, Sushi, Chinese, Japanese, Thai, Mexican, Greek, and Polish cuisine. Classes are typically offered on weeknights.

Cooking Resources

ChicagoCooks.com

www.chicagocooks.com

Slow Food

www.slowfoodusa.org

Dance, *Dance,* *in the City!*

Authentic Middle East Belly Dance

PO Box 56037
Chicago, IL 60656
Ph. 773-693-6300/Fax 773-693-6302
www.jasminjahal.com

This is the place to be if you've ever wanted to learn the exotic art of belly dancing. Authentic Middle East Belly Dance was founded by Jasmin Jahal to teach Westerners the art of belly dance. Classes include Level I - Basic Belly Dance Techniques, Level II - Choreography, and Level III – Advanced, which is geared towards students serious about pursuing belly dance professionally. Also offered is Belly Aerobics, which combines the art of belly dance with a great workout. Classes are offered in the City and suburbs.

Belle Plaine Studio

2014 W. Belle Plaine
Chicago, IL 60618
Ph. 773-935-1890/Fax 773-935-1909

The Belle Plaine Studio offers a variety of dance and yoga classes in a newly renovated historic building on the North side of Chicago. Dance classes include Middle Eastern Belly Dance, Contemporary Dance, Ballet, Flamenco, Hip Hop, and Tap. Yoga and Pilates are also offered. Classes are offered in the evening during the week and on weekends.

Chicago Dance

3660 W. Irving Park Rd.
Chicago, IL 60618
Ph. 773-267-3411/Fax 773-267-1084
www.chicagodance.com

Founded in 1976, Chicago Dance offers a wide variety of dance classes such as Latin, Salsa, Cha Cha, Argentine Tango, Swing, and Fox Trot. The school's multi-cultural student body is made up of over 500 active students, ages 8 to 90, which can make classes very interesting and fun. There's also another location in Chicago on West Huron.

Joel Hall Dance Center

1511 West Berwyn
Chicago, IL 60640
Ph. 773-293-0900
www.joelhall.org

The Joel Hall Dance Center is one of the most diverse dance studios in the City. The mission of the dance center is to enrich people's lives through dance. A wide variety of classes are held daily including Jazz, Ballet I-III, Lyrical Jazz, Jazz Hip Hop, Beginning Tap, Belly Dance, Salsa, and more. Levels range from beginner to advanced. Classes are held throughout the day, in the evenings, and on weekends.

Latin Street Dancing

540 N. LaSalle St., Suite 500
Chicago, IL 60610
Ph. 312-42-SALSA/312-427-2572
Fax 312-527-9238
www.laboriqua.com

This dance studio is "hot" in every sense of the word. If you've ever wanted to learn how to Salsa, this is the place to go. Latin Street Dancing offers Meringue, Cha Cha, Argentine Tango, Chicago Mambo, Batchata, and a lot more. With over 8,000 square feet of dance space, and over a dozen dance instructors, this is an ideal place to add a little spice to your life and dash of rhythm to your step.

Natya Dance Theatre

410 South Michigan Ave., Suite 725
Chicago, IL 60605
Ph. 312-212-1240/Fax 312-212-1250
www.natya.com

Founded in 1975, Natya Dance Theatre teaches its students the classical dance of India called Bharata Natyam. This dance has been in existence for about 2,000 years and has played an integral role in India's culture. Class levels offered range from beginner to advanced. Classes are held in Chicago, Schaumburg, Oakbrook, and Lombard during the week in the evenings and on weekends.

McDonald Dance Academy

34 S. Evergreen
Arlington Heights, IL 60005
Ph. 847-342-1060
www.mcdonalddance.com

The McDonald Dance Academy places high emphasis on correct dance skills and technique. Here, dancers are taught the theory and terminology needed to excel in dance. The academy welcomes beginners as well as advanced students to its Ballet, Jazz, Funk, Modern, and Tap classes. Pointe classes are specifically offered to advanced students. Pilates is offered to help dancers of all levels hone their skills.

The School of Ballet Chicago

218 S. Wabash St., 3rd Fl
Chicago, IL 60604
Ph. 312-251-8838/Fax 312-251-8840
www.balletchicago.org

The School of Ballet Chicago, which offers ballet classes to both adults and children, is a great place to learn the art of ballet. Instructors are highly motivated, encouraging, and enthusiastic, which tends to rub off on the students. The mission of this organization is to develop future professional classical dancers. In addition to this, the school seeks to provide quality training to those who enjoy the art, but do not wish to pursue ballet on a professional level. Adults, who simply love ballet and want to obtain the benefits of better poise, self-confidence, and discipline, have the option of taking classes on a drop-in basis.

Languages & Cultures

in the City!

Alliance Française de Chicago

810 N. Dearborn St.
Chicago, IL 60610
Ph. 312-337-1070
Fax 312-337-3019
www.afchicago.com

This is the place to go if you want to learn French and have fun while you're doing it. Alliance Française de Chicago is a cultural organization dedicated to promoting the French language and culture throughout the world. There are over 1,200 chapters of this organization in 138 countries with 137 chapters currently existing in the United States. Alliance Française de Chicago offers very lively French classes such as French for Travelers, Understanding Spoken French through Film, Hot off the French Press, Conversation, Debat, et Discussion, Grammaire en Conversation, and more. Classes that prepare students for French proficiency exams are also available. In addition to language classes, this organization offers French cooking instruction, a film club, and a poetry-reading group. Alliance Française de Chicago also holds several cultural events throughout the year featuring art, music, film, literature, theatre, and lectures.

French Institute of the North Shore

562 Green Bay Rd.
Winnetka, IL 60093
Ph. 847-501-5800/Fax 847-501-5855
www.FrenchInstituteNS.com

The French Institute of the North Shore is dedicated to furthering the French language and culture. Classes are limited to only 12 students, which makes them friendly, intimate, highly interactive, and fun. Teachers use props and real life scenarios to put students in that "French" state of mind. This teaching method along with the French décor helps students increase their comprehension of the language. Classes, which range from beginner to advanced, are offered in ten-week sessions. Audio programs and immersion workshops are available to further enhance learning.

French Accents

3755 N. Western Ave.
Chicago, IL 60618
Ph. 773-490-2141
www.frenchaccents.org

French Accents is a newer organization that teaches and promotes French language and culture. This organization takes a non-traditional approach to learning French. Classes are lively and instructors make students feel comfortable. Class sessions last for ten weeks and range from beginner to advanced. Average class sizes range from 4-10 people to ensure personal attention.

Spanish Circle

10 W. Hubbard St., Suite 3E
Chicago, IL 60610
Ph. 312-832-1282 or 773-525-9808
www.spanishcircle.com

If you'd like to learn Spanish or build upon what you've already learned, check out Spanish Circle. This language school takes a different approach to learning Spanish. Instead of the typical memorization, this school teaches its students to think and express themselves in Spanish from the beginning. Class sizes are small (6-12 students) to ensure maximum interaction. Sessions last for six weeks and take place during the day, in the evenings, and on weekends. Also, there are two Chicago locations—one in River North and the other in Lakeview.

Spanish Horizons

2526 N. Lincoln Ave., Ste 219
Chicago, IL 60614
Ph. 773-769-6300/773-348-7686
Fax 773-348-8518
www.spanishhorizons.com

Spanish Horizons offers a variety of classes suitable for both professionals and students alike. Classes at this Lincoln Park language school range from beginner to intermediate and typically include 4 - 6 students. Private and semi-private lessons are also available in Lincoln Park or at a student's location of choice. The environment is friendly, intimate and professional. Courses run in eight-week sessions that meet two hours a week. Evening and weekend classes are available. Parking is free, which is a huge plus in Chicago. Translation and interpretation services are also offered.

Instituto Cervantes Chicago

875 N. Michigan Ave. Suite 2940
Chicago, IL 60611
Ph. 312-335-1996/Fax 312-587-1992
www.cervantes1.org

Located in the John Hancock Center, Instituto Cervantes Chicago offers Spanish language and cultural classes and activities. The institute also promotes Spanish arts, music, literature, theatre, and cinema. Spanish language classes range from beginner to advanced and even prepare students to obtain certificates such as the Certificate of Spanish as a Second Language. Spanish for business courses are also offered for students who use the language in their professional lives. Class sizes are limited to 12 students and 30 hours of instruction is typically given over a ten-week period. Online classes are also available. Other opportunities to learn Spanish include lunch conversation groups, lecture series, conferences, and literature groups.

Spanish Studios

722 W. Diversey Ave.
Chicago, IL 60614
Ph. 773-348-2216/Fax 773-435-2119
www.spanishstudio.com

Spanish Studios has been providing language instruction for 30 years. Classes offered include beginning to advanced Spanish, Italian, Portuguese and English. Both group and private lessons are offered in three locations—Lincoln Park, Hyde Park, and West Lakeview. Off-site classes can also be arranged. Other activities include field trips to Chicago's Latino communities, ethnic restaurants, and museums. Spanish Studios also offers local immersion weekends, and a conversational Spanish gourmet club.

Intrax English Institute

174 N. Michigan Ave., 2nd Fl
Chicago, IL 60601
Ph. 312-236-3208/Fax 312-236-3246
www.intraxenglish.com

Intrax English Institute offers English as a Second Language classes for those who wish to improve their English. This language school prepares its students to take the TOEFL (Test of English as a Foreign Language) exam. There are 10 different proficiency levels from beginner to high proficient. Courses are supplemented with free workshops offered on Fridays and class sizes range from 12-15 students. The facilities are equipped with computer labs where students have both Internet and e-mail access. Certificate programs and internships are also available.

Italidea

500 N. Michigan Ave.
Chicago, IL 60611
Ph. 312-832-4053/Fax 312-822-9622
www.italidea.org

Italidea offers Italian language courses for beginners as well as advanced students. Class sizes are small and highly interactive. Instructors are native Italians with degrees from Italian universities. An intensive course for beginners planning to go to Italy is offered as well as a conversational course for advanced students. In addition to language classes, Italidea offers classes in cooking, wine, and opera. All three sets of courses are taught in both English and Italian.

Take A Class! In the City

Japanese Culture Center

1016 W. Belmont Ave.
Chicago, IL 60657
Ph. 773-525-3141/Fax 773-525-5916
www.japaneseculturecenter.com

The Japanese Culture Center offers a variety Japanese language and art classes in addition to instruction in martial arts. Classes are typically offered seven days a week in Chicago, Palatine, and Burbank.

Philosophy, Social Science & Writing
in the City!

The Henry George School of Social Science

417 S. Dearborn, Suite 510
Chicago, IL 60605
Ph. 312-362-9302
www.hgchicago.org

Located in the South Loop, The Henry George School is a non-profit organization dedicated to educating adults about economics, poverty, injustice, and environmental problems. Classes are based on several works by Henry George, a popular economist from the late 1800's. Classes, such as Progress and Poverty, Protection of Free Trade, and Social Problems, typically meet once a week for 90 minutes over a 6-10 week period. In most cases, classes are free with the exception of a $10 registration fee.

Newberry Library

60 W. Walton St.
Chicago, IL 60610
Ph. 312-255-3700/Fax 312-255-3680
www.newberry.org

The Newberry Library specializes in humanities and is open to the public. This unique library holds exhibits and author-led book discussions. If you are interested in researching your family history, this library has a membership group called Friends of Genealogy (FOG) that can offer support. FOG activities include lectures, networking, and a monthly writing group called Preserving Memories. There is also another group called the Wednesday Club that offers presentations on Wednesday evenings designed to spark conversation and discussion. The Newberry Library also offers seminars and classes on a variety of topics including writing and literature.

The Feltre School

22 W. Erie St.
Chicago, IL 60610
Ph. 312-255-1133/Fax 312-255-1378
www.feltre.org

Founded in 1992, the Feltre School is a private, non-profit school that specializes in liberal arts for the professional or continuing education student. Classes offered at the Feltre School include English Grammar, Writing, Public Speaking, Humanities, Logic and Mathematics, Philosophy, and Latin. There is also a reading group that meets once a month to discuss renowned literary works like Brave New World, A Street Car Named Desire, and Their Eyes Were Watching God.

Guild Complex

1532 N. Milwaukee Ave.
Chicago, IL 60622
Ph. 773-227-6117/Fax 773-227-6159
www.guildcomplex.com

The Guild Complex is a non-profit cultural organization that offers literary workshops and seminars in a variety of genres including poetry, fiction, non-fiction, humor, and playwriting. Literary discussions are also facilitated throughout the year. This is a great organization for aspiring writers because its publishing arm, Tia Chucha Press, has published 32 Chicago authors to date.

Writers Digest School/WritersOnlineWorkshop.com

4700 E. Galbraith Rd.
Cincinnati, OH 45236
Ph. 1-800-759-0963
www.writersdigest.com/wds

Okay, Okay…they're not exactly located in Chicago, (they're located in Cincinnati) but if you have Internet access, they're right at your fingertips. The Writers Digest School offers courses to aspiring as well as experienced writers. Students complete writing assignments and mail them to the instructors, who are published authors, for critiquing. Courses offered through this home study writing program include Getting Started in Writing, Fundamentals of Fiction Workshop, Fundamentals of Non-Fiction Workshop, The Elements of Effective Writing I&II, Writing & Selling Non-Fiction Articles, Writing & Selling Short Stories, and The Novel Writing Workshop.

WritingClasses.com (Gotham Writer's Workshop)

1841 Broadway, Suite 809
New York, NY 10023
Ph. 877-WRITERS
Fax 212-307-6325
www.writingclasses.com

This organization isn't based in Chicago either, but like Writers Digest School, it's just a mouse click away. WritingClasses.com describes itself as "New York's no-nonsense writing school." If you're serious about taking your writing to the next level, check out on-line (and offline) classes and seminars such as Fiction Writing, Memoir Writing, Non-Fiction, Screenwriting, Novel Writing, Songwriting, Writing for Business, Sitcom Writing, Stand-up Comedy Writing, Romance Writing, and more.

StoryStudio Chicago

3717 N. Ravenswood, Suite 115
Chicago, IL 60613
Ph. 773-728-8441
www.storystudiochicago.com

The Story Studio is an organization dedicated to the development and support of writers. This new organization offers classes and workshops in areas such as creative writing, poetry, and business writing. There are also other writing related events and services such as book discussions, personalized instruction, and coaching.

Music in the City!

Allegro Music Studio

5301 N. Clark St.
Chicago, IL 60640
Ph. 773-334-4650
www.allegromusicstudio.com

Located in the historic Andersonville section of Chicago, Allegro Music Studio offers instruction in piano. Lessons are held year round, and range from 30 minutes to 60 minutes. Specific instruction includes Theory, History, Ear Training, and Sight Reading. A free consultation is offered to prospective students. Other activities and events include student recitals and competitions.

Bloom School of Jazz

218 S. Wabash Ave., Suite 600
Chicago, IL 60640
Ph. 312-957-9300/Fax 312-957-0133
www.bloomschoolofjazz.com

The Bloom School of Jazz has been teaching beginning to advanced jazz students for over 25 years. Students attending this music school come from all walks of life. The mixture of ethnic and socioeconomic backgrounds and wide spectrum of ages add to the School's uniqueness. Classes offered include Intro to Jazz, Music Theory & Ear Training, Jazz Awareness, Jazz Vocals, and more. Special courses include the Jazz Artist Program that lasts for one year and is designed to help students find their own musical voice within the art of Jazz. Another special program that lasts for 6 months is called

Take A Class! In the City

The Perfect Set. This program, taught by David Bloom himself, is very demanding and challenges students in the areas of composition, arranging, and improvisation. Private instruction and seminars are also offered.

Old Town School of Folk Music

4544 N. Lincoln Ave.
Chicago, IL 60625
Ph. 773-728-6000
www.oldtownschool.org

The Old Town School of Folk Music opened its doors in 1957 when its primary emphasis was on folk music. Today, the school prides itself on teaching a diverse array of musical traditions including jazz and blues. There are over 6,000 students enrolled at this music school with about 4,000 of them being adults. Group adult instruction categories include Banjo, Bass, Blues, Cello, Dance, Ensembles, Fiddle, Guitar, Harmonica, Jazz, Mandolin, Percussion, Reeds & Wind, Song Writing, Theatre, Music Theory, Ukulele, and Voice. Private instruction is also available in most of these categories. Classes are conveniently offered in the evenings and on weekends at two Chicago locations.

The People's Music School

931 W. Eastwood
Chicago, IL 60640
Ph. 773-784-7032/Fax 773-784-7134
www.peoplesmusicschool.org

The People's Music School was founded in 1976 so that people could have access to classical music education. The School chose its Uptown location because of its ethnic diversity. Classes are free (with the exception of a $10 registration fee) and open to both children and adults. The School offers music theory classes as well as an instructional program. Areas of study include Piano, Strings, Woodwinds, Brass, Percussion, Guitar, and Voice.

Adult *Continuing* Education *in the City!*

The Discovery Center

2940 N. Lincoln Ave.
Chicago, IL 60657
Ph. 773-348-8120
www.discoverycenter.cc

Have you ever wanted to learn something new for the sheer fun of learning without worrying about grades or exams? If the answer is yes, then check out the Discovery Center. This organization has been around for just over 25 years and is one of Chicago's largest independent adult continuing education programs. Classes are available for the mild and the wild. You can learn just about anything at the Discovery Center. Class categories include Acting, Arts and Crafts, Dance, Theatre, Languages, Real Estate, Photography, Sports and Recreation, Business and Careers, and much more. If you're single, the Discovery Center also hosts relationship seminars, speed-dating parties, and singles mixers.

The Graham School

1427 East 60th St.
Chicago, IL 60637
Ph. 773-702-1722
www.grahamschool.uchicago.edu

The University of Chicago (U of C) is one of the world's finest institutions of higher learning. In addition to offering some of the best degree programs, U of C offers a top-notch adult continuing education program. If you're simply looking for stimulating conversation about a wide range of topics, the Graham School offers a credit and non-credit Liberal Arts & Sciences program. Areas of study include African & African-American studies, Art History, Drama & Theatre, Languages, Leadership Studies/Human Development, Music, Personal Investing, Philosophy, Political Science, Psychology, Speech Communication, and Women's Studies. There's also a writer's studio for those interested in writing, editing, and publishing. For those who wish to combine travel and education, U of C has a travel study program that has visited places such as Africa, London, and New York. The Graham School is also ideal for anyone wishing to take their career to the next level. The Business & Professional Program offers courses in Marketing, IT Strategy, Management, Career & Life Strategies, & much more. Both credit & non-credit courses are available.

The Norris Center at Northwestern University

1999 S. Campus Dr.
Evanston, IL 60208
Ph. 847-491-2301
http://www.norris.northwestern.edu/nmc_main.php

The Norris Center at Northwestern University offers a Mini Course Program that consists of non-credit courses. Courses are offered in Dance, Music, Photography, Fine Arts & Crafts, Languages, Writing, Literature, Yoga, Martial Arts, Wine Appreciation, and Pool. Classes are affordable and typically offered during the week in the evenings.

Take A Class! In the City

Oakton Community College

1600 E. Golf Rd.
Des Plaines, IL 60016
Ph. 847-635-1600
www.oakton.edu

Oakton Community College (OCC) offers adult continuing education classes through its Alliance for Lifelong Learning (A.L.L.) division. Each semester, thousands of students take advantage of literally hundreds of classes offered at the Des Plaines and Skokie Campuses, as well as surrounding high schools. A.L.L. class categories include Around the Home (Home Improvement, Interior Decorating); Arts and Culture (Drawing, Painting, Sculpture, Pottery, Music, Theatre); Automotive (Small Engine Repair); Business (Starting a Small Business, Business Writing, Marketing, Financial Planning); Dance & Fitness (Ballroom, Latin Dancing, Aerobics, Personal Training); Life Enrichment & Wellness (CPR, First Aid, Nutrition, Health, Personal Development); Online Instruction (Accounting, Starting a Business, Writing, MS Word, Excel, PowerPoint, Access); Web Page Design (Photoshop, Java Programming, Intro. to the Internet); Real Estate (Real Estate Classes, Real Estate Continuing Education); Sports & Recreation (Fishing, Golfing, Sailing, Scuba Diving, Volleyball). International travel courses are also offered.

Harper College

1200 W. Algonquin Rd.
Palatine, IL 60067
Ph. 847-925-6300
www.harpercollege.edu

Harper College offers over 500 classes through its Continuing Education program. Classes are very interactive and led by instructors who have real life experience with the subjects they teach. Two major program categories include Professional Development and Personal Enrichment. The Personal Enrichment program offers popular classes in Home Arts (Cooking, Woodworking, Decorating, Gardening and Landscaping); Physical Fitness & Wellness (Volleyball, Basketball, Salsa and Swing); Communication (The Art of Conversation and Great First and Lasting Impressions); Money Management (Financial Planning, Stock Market Strategies Managing Credit and Debt); New Age (Yoga, Reiki, T'ai Chi Ch'uan, Unmasking Your Dreams); Music (private instruction in Voice, Strings, Guitar, Flute, Saxophone, Clarinet, Trumpet, and Percussion and group instruction in String Ensembles for Adults). Professional Development courses include Certified Financial Planning, International Trade, Customs Entry Writer Certification, Meeting and Event Planning, Volunteer Management, Web Maintenance & Design, and a whole host of other professional certificate programs and courses.

Moraine Valley Community College

10900 S. 88th Ave.
Palos Hills, IL 60465
Ph. 708-974-4300
www.morainevalley.edu

Moraine Valley College offers hundreds of personal and professional development classes to South suburban communities. Class categories include Basic Skills (English as a Second Language, GED); Career Training (Computer Software and Technical Training); Foreign Languages (Spanish, Spanish for specific occupations); First Aid & CPR, Continuing Education for Teachers, Hospitality Instruction, Management and Professional Skills, and Real Estate. Personal Enrichment courses include Health, Fitness, Sports, Home Improvement, Personal Finance, Languages, and Older Adult Programs.

City Colleges of Chicago

Ph. 773-COLLEGE
www.ccc.edu

The continuing education classes offered by the City Colleges of
Chicago vary depending on the location. You can take classes in
a wide variety of areas including cooking, dancing, business, and
theatre. The City Colleges are located throughout the City of Chicago
and include Richard M. Daley College, Harold Washington College,
Malcolm X College, Olive-Harvey College, Harry S. Truman College,
Kennedy King College, and Wright College.

Prairie State College

202 S. Halstead St.
Chicago Heights, IL 60411
Ph. 708-709-3500
www.prairie.cc.il.us

Prairie State College has been serving the South suburbs since
1958. This college, which has locations in Chicago Heights and
Matteson offers a wide variety of continuing education and personal
development classes in categories such as Arts & Crafts (Stained
Glass, Acrylic Painting, Drawing, Watercolor, Quilting, Basket
Weaving); Business (Communication Skills, The Skills of Negotiation,
Grant Writing); Dance (Line Dancing, Stepping, Latin Dance, Belly
Dance); Computers (Front Page, Dreamweaver, Quickbooks); Cooking
(Italian, Breadmaking, Food Service Operation); Home Improvement
(Plumbing, Do It Yourself Room Building); Interior Design (Painting,
Decorating, Wall Stenciling); Languages (Sign Language, Spanish);
Sports & Fitness (Tai Chi, Pilates, Walking, Aerobics, Golf); and a lot
more.

College of DuPage

425 Fawell Blvd.
Glen Ellyn, IL 60137
Ph. 630-942-2208
www.cod.edu

The College of DuPage is one of the largest community colleges in the state. It offers a wide variety of Continuing Education classes in the areas of Arts and Crafts (painting, calligraphy, jewelry making, photography); Home Improvement (interior decorating, feng shui, gardening, flower arranging, Culinary Arts (basic cooking skills, nutrition, wine tasting); Personal Development (travel, culture, religions, healthy living); Life Enhancement (sports and fitness, hobby and recreation, image and beauty); and Foreign Languages (Arabic, Chinese, Japanese, Polish, Portuguese, French, Spanish, sign-language.)

Personal Growth & Self-Help in the City!

Wright Institute for Lifelong Learning

455 E. Ohio St., Suite 260
Chicago, IL 60611
Ph. 312-329-1200/Fax 312-645-8333
www.exceptionalliving.com

The Wright Institute for Lifelong Learning is a place to develop your "whole" self. This very unique organization offers personal enrichment courses as well as individual coaching in the areas of Spirituality, Careers, Relationships, and Self. The school believes we are given gifts to develop and that we have lessons to learn while here on earth. It also believes that by developing our gifts, we can move upward in consciousness. The school holds local classes and other programs in downtown Chicago as well as retreats in beautiful Elkhorn, Wisconsin.

Innerconnections

708 Church St., Suite 258
Evanston, IL 60201
Ph. 847-864-3730/Fax 847-256-8150
www.innerconnections.cc

Innerconnections offers two courses—The Artist's Way and
Continuing the Journey. Both these courses are based on Julia
Cameron's books *The Artist Way: A Spiritual Path to Higher Creativity*
and run 13 and 8 weeks respectively. These classes are for anyone
who has the desire to take a creative approach to examining as well as
living their lives.

Institute for Spiritual Leadership

5498 S. Kimbark
PO Box 53147
Chicago, IL 60653
Ph. 877-844-9440/Fax 773-752-5964
www.spiritleader.org

The Institute for Spiritual Leadership has been training students in the
area of Christian spirituality for 25 years. Programs combine personal
development and professional development and include courses
such as Personal Transformation Mission, Dreamwork, Paths and
Practices, and Contemplative Attitude. Certain age and educational
requirements must be met in order to be admitted. Weekday and
weekend programs are available.

Get Buff!

Running

Biking

Ski

Sailing

Kayak

Canoeing

Martial Arts

Triathalon

Training

Marathon

Kickboxing

Snowboard

Leagues

Get Buff! In The City

Chicago and most of the surrounding suburbs offer literally hundreds of opportunities to Get Buff! We are indeed an active city, taking full advantage of our parks, beaches, and bike paths. There's always a ton of races and other athletic events going on in both the City and the suburbs throughout the year. There's also a number of clubs you can join if you enjoy or want to learn more about a particular sport. If you simply want to achieve your fitness goals, Chicago also has its fair share of training programs that can help you to succeed.

In the spring of 2001, I decided to complete a marathon. I had done a few 5-k and 10-k races and was ready to take on a new challenge. My goal was to simply complete a 26.2 mile race. I wasn't obsessed with how long it would take to complete the marathon; I just wanted to finish the race without injury. To date, I have completed 2 marathons and a half marathon. I have also completed an indoor triathlon. If you have the desire to take on a challenge such as a marathon or any other type of physical competition, hold onto your desire and remember what your personal goal is if and when your training gets tough. For me, the real victory is being fit and healthy. I have diabetes and training for these competitions gives me another more positive reason to lead an active healthy lifestyle. My main goal for getting buff is being able to lead an active healthy lifestyle without diabetes complications.

We all can benefit from getting buff. Staying active is fun, keeps your stress levels low and can be a great way to meet people in Chicago.

So, whether your goal is to get a 6-pack run a marathon, ride your bike more often, or to simply have a great time while keeping fit, there's bound to be a club, league, training program, or fitness group that's perfect for you.

Chicago Hash House Harriers

3155 N. Hudson
Chicago, IL, 60657
Ph. 312-409-BEER (2337)
www.chicagohash.com

Wild, crazy, and fun are three words that best describe the Chicago Hash House Harriers. This group usually meets weekly for fun runs throughout the City and suburbs. These weekly runs are truly like no other. In fact, every run is different—always taking place in a new location. Here's how it works. Every week, a member is appointed to be a "hare" or "harriette". The hare or harriette plans and marks a trail. The "hashers" (the rest of the runners) follow this trail either running, walking or jogging. After the runs, the hashers reward themselves with beer and grub at a local pub. In addition to being wild, crazy, and fun, this running group probably has the most interesting history. It all began in 1938 by a group of British expatriate businessmen in Kuala Lumpur, Malaysia. The name Hash House Harriers comes from a nickname they gave to the place they lived and dined at the time. The concept of a hare marking a trail and hashers following comes from an old game played in Britain by young schoolboys. There are now over 1,700 active clubs worldwide with over 350 in the U.S.

Chicago Walkers Club

2909 N. Sheridan Rd., Suite 1707
Chicago, IL 60657
Ph. 773-348-3891
http://sekelsky.com/chicagowalkers

If running is a bit of a stretch for you, why not try walking? This is the ideal group for anyone just beginning an exercise program. Remember the old saying, "You've gotta walk before your run?" The Chicago Walkers Club teaches race walking for fun and fitness. Members are of all walking and fitness levels and range in age from 9-80. This group is so much fun that folks come from many miles away to enjoy weekly 5-k race walks followed by breakfast and socializing at a local restaurant.

Fleet Feet Running Groups

210 W. North Ave.
Chicago, IL 60610
Ph. 312-587-3338
www.fleetfeetchicago.com

Fleet Feet Sports has several running groups that meet throughout the week at two of their retail locations. Twice a week, Fleet Feet hosts 3-8 mile fun runs in the evenings. On Tuesdays there are fun runs for women only. One of the best things about these running groups is that they are free to the public. All you do is show up and run. Runners of all levels participate in these weekly fun runs. There are also seminars after each run on various fitness and running topics including nutrition, hydration, and running techniques.

Frontrunners/Frontwalkers Chicago

PO Box 148313
Chicago, IL 60614
Ph. 312-409-2790
www.frfwchicago.org

Frontrunners/Frontwalkers Chicago (FRFW) is very social and active running club serving gays and lesbians interested in keeping physically fit and socializing. FRFW Chicago is part of a larger international organization with over 30 chapters in several countries including Great Britain, Canada, Australia, Japan, Israel, and South Africa. In the U.S. you can find a club in all major cities. The Chicago chapter is a very diverse group with over 350 members some of whom serve on the Chicago Area Runners Association (CARA) advisory board as well as the editorial board of CARA's magazine Chicago Runner. Every week, this group has fun runs and walks along the lakefront. Afterwards, many members go to a nearby restaurant to enjoy a meal. This club also organizes monthly socials and volunteer events for their members. Some past events and activities include game nights, film outings, wine tasting, and dining. This fun and lively group also has an annual holiday party in December and a picnic in July. *Frontpages*, a monthly newsletter, keeps members informed of races, social activities, and other topics of interest.

Lincoln Park Pacers

PO Box 14835
Chicago, IL 60614
Ph. 773-472-2344
www.lincolnparkpacers.org

Fun and lively describe the Lincoln Park Pacers. This group meets twice per week for fun runs that can range from 3-5k. After each run, the group usually meets for a meal at a local restaurant. Runs generally take place in Lincoln Park or along the lakefront. In addition to running, the Pacers also enjoy social activities such as Ethnic Dinners and parties.

Life Time Fitness Running Clubs

www.lifetimefitness.com
Located in the North, South and West suburbs

Life Time Fitness, one of the most down to earth, exclusive suburban health clubs chains, has running clubs that cater to both experienced and novice runners who are members of the health club. The goal of the club is to provide information and support to those who want to incorporate running into their fitness routines. Benefits include group and special holiday runs, information and tips on running gear, and a fun social setting. Clubs vary by location.

Alpine Runners

Ph. 847-438-8843
www.alpinerunners.com

The Alpine Runners Club is based in the Northwest suburb of Lake Zurich. It has over 500 members and is always looking for more people who would like to improve their health as well as maintain an active lifestyle. This group offers training runs and fun runs several times during the week. The Alpine Runners has something for runners of all abilities—from the beginner to the experienced marathoner. They also host a marathon-training program as well as programs for beginning runners. Running distances generally vary from 4.5 miles all the way up to 22 miles. This group has also sponsored races such as the 2001 Snow Fun Run, the Great Western 30k, and the Chicago and Nashville Marathons.

Hillstriders Running Club

PO Box 1695
Crystal Lake, IL 60039
Ph. 815-455-4290
www.hillstriders.com

The Hillstriders Running Club is located in the far Northwest suburbs of Cary and Crystal Lake. This group is made up of people who enjoy running—from the beginner to the novice. Fun runs are held regularly around the village of Crystal Lake. The Hillstriders are a very social group, often enjoying pizza after runs. Every year, the Hillstriders sponsor the March Madness Half Marathon where club members volunteer their time to make the race a success. A newsletter is also sent to club members to keep them abreast of important dates and activities.

Fox River Trail Runners

PO Box 371
Geneva, IL 60134
Ph. 630-208-6677
www.frtr.org

The mission of the Fox River Trail Runners is to promote running for fun and lifetime fitness. This running group is six years old and has 300 members who come from all over the state of Illinois. Fox River Trail Runners enjoy weekly runs as well as track workouts. A monthly newsletter called *Foxtales* goes out to club members detailing important club news and social activities. Other club benefits include club uniforms, club sponsored races, and access to coaches.

Lisle Windrunners

PO Box 1171
Lisle, IL 60532
Ph. 630-585-4695
www.windrunners.org

The Lisle Windrunners, located in the Western suburbs, is a group of about 75 running enthusiasts who meet regularly for runs that range anywhere between 5 and 10 miles. Members run for the pure enjoyment of running. Many runners do, however, compete in races—from 5k to marathons. The club holds regular meetings to discuss club business as well as running topics. A club newsletter informs members of upcoming activities, important dates, and member achievements. This club is a member of CARA and the Road Runners Club of America.

Park Forest Running & Pancake Club

PO Box 442
Park Forest, IL 60466
Ph. 708-802-2759
www.lincolnnet.net/pfrpc

Founded in 1978, the Park Forest Running and Pancake Club is based in the South suburbs and has members that come from the Chicagoland area and Northwest Indiana. This group is active all year round and sponsors races, fun runs, speed workouts, training runs, moon runs, road trips, and lots of social gatherings. This running group welcomes runners (and walkers) of all abilities.

Evanston Running Club

PO Box 5329
Evanston, IL 60201
Ph. 847-869-8234

The Evanston Running Club is a group of runners with diverse backgrounds and running abilities. This running club meets once a week for group runs with the first fun run of each month being followed by dinner at an Evanston restaurant. Other member benefits include a bi-monthly newsletter, a T-shirt, and admission into three parties every year.

Arlington Trotters Running Club

Ph. 847-670-8331 or 847-368-0887
www.geocities.com/arltrotter

The Arlington Trotters running club serves runners of all abilities. Its mission is to "support each member in achieving his or her individual running goals." The club, which has over 250 members, is a great support system for achieving fitness as well as competitive running goals. It's also a great avenue for making friends. The Arlington Trotters has several fun runs throughout the week led by its members. Monthly club meetings allow guest speakers and members to discuss a variety of fitness and running topics (meetings are not held during the summer months). A club newsletter called the *Trotter* is produced to keep abreast of club news and activities. Social opportunities include dinners, beer runs, post race parties, and more.

Oak Park Runners Club

PO Box 2322
Oak Park, IL 60304
Ph. 708-848-3365
www.oprc.net

The Oak Park Runner's Club (OPRC) welcomes anyone who has a passion and enthusiasm for running. Whether you're young or old, a veteran runner or a beginner, this club has something to offer you. The club hosts Monday Night Fun runs that are shorter distance fun runs (5-10 miles) as well as Saturday morning Fun runs that are longer distances (10-20 miles). OPRC members have monthly meetings where experts are invited to discuss training techniques, injury prevention, shoe selection, and more. There is also an annual awards banquet to recognize key members and a newsletter called *Foot Notes* that keeps OPRC members abreast of club activities.

Polish Marathon Club of Chicago

Ph. 708-583-0494 or 708-583-0574
www.marathonpl.com

Members of the Polish Marathon Club of Chicago are a group of people who share a common heritage as well as a common passion for running. Their goal is"…to enhance Polonia's sports culture and to energize active runners and encourage new competitors." Members run marathons on every continent. All people with a passion for running and a desire to learn more about the Polish culture are welcome.

Lake Forest-Lake Bluff Running Club

www.lflb.org

For over 22 years, the Lake Forest-Lake Bluff Running Club has organized weekly group runs and walks for members of varying abilities. The main group run takes place on Saturday morning, but other runs—the long (16 miles) and the short (6 miles) occur throughout the week. In addition to running and walking, club members enjoy other activities such as biking, Ravinia nights, parties, and races. There is also a club newsletter called *Footprints* that informs members of club information and activities.

Niles West/Oakton Runners Club

www.nileswestoaktonrunnersclub.com

Founded and coached by Pat and Melissa Savage, the Niles West/ Oakton Runners Club is a club for runners of all abilities who not only enjoy running, but who also want to improve their skills. These coaches are very experienced runners who impart their knowledge and expertise to club members. Track work outs are held once per week at Niles West High School. Other club activities include an annual dinner banquet, the annual Pub Run, and volunteering at many races including the Chicago Marathon.

RunBig Chicago

www.orik.com/runbig
PO Box 1826
Oak Park, IL 60304-1826

RunBig Chicago is a multi-sport fitness club for Clydesdale athletes. Clydesdale athletes are bigger than the average athlete—over 170lbs for men and over 135lbs for women. This club, among others such as the Clydesdale Runners Association, promotes weight division competitions so that Clydesdales athletes obtain the recognition they deserve in races among their peers. Membership benefits include participation in RunBig race circuits, an e-newsletter, free clinics, group runs, swims, club meetings, parties, and award ceremonies.

Get Buff! Running
Resources!
In the City!

CARA

203 N.Wabash Ave., Suite 1104
Chicago, IL 60601
Ph. 312-666-9836
www.cararuns.org

If you are an avid runner or would like to become one, CARA is the place to start. One of the largest running organizations in the Midwest, CARA sponsors a variety of races, clinics, training programs, and running clubs throughout the city and suburbs. Whether you want to run a marathon or a 5-k race, CARA has a program just for you. CARA training programs include Beginning Running, Marathon & Half Marathon Training, 5-k, 10-k, and 8-k Training, Speed Training, Peak Performance, and Gait Analysis. CARA also offers running related clinics that cover a variety of topics including shoe selection, hydration, goal setting, running safety, and much, much, more. Participating in CARA events, fun runs, or CARA running clubs is a great way to meet people who enjoy running as much as you do.

RRCA—Road Runners Club America

510 N. Washington St.
Alexandria, VA 22314
Ph. 703-836-0558
www.rrca.org

The Road Runners Club America (RRCA) is a national association made up of running clubs and individuals dedicated to promoting the benefits of long distance running. There are over 600 running clubs and over 130,000 members who are a part of this organization. The RRCA provides education and leadership programs tailored to the needs of runners at all levels. It publishes *Footnotes*, the third largest running publication in the nation, as well as educational materials for women and children runners. This organization also provides information on how to start a running club. Check out rrca.org for a listing of member running groups in the Chicago area.

AATRA—All American Trail Running Association

PO Box 9454
Colorado Springs, CO 80932
www.trailrunner.com
719-573-440

The All American Trail Running Association (AATRA) is a national organization dedicated to promoting trail and mountain running. If you're looking to take your running off the pavement and into the mountains or the forest trails, this association is the place to start. The AATRA Web site contains information about various clubs and races for those interested in this genre of running.

American Running Association

4405 E. West Hwy, Suite 405
Bethesda, MD 20814
Ph. 1-800-776-2732
www.americanrunning.org

The American Running Association (ARA) offers a variety of programs and services for runners of all levels. Its mission is to "… encourage people to improve their health and fitness by running and maintaining an active and healthy lifestyle." Over 15,000 members currently benefit ARA programs.

Running USA

5522 Camino Cerrallo
Santa Barbara, CA 93111
Ph. 805-964-060
www.runningusa.org

Founded in 1999, Running USA is a non-profit organization dedicated to promoting road racing and long distance running. To achieve its objective, Running USA partners with USA Track and Field and road racing associations to produce hundreds of events, road racing and long distance running.

USA Track & Field

1 RCA Dome Ste. 140
Indianapolis, IN 46225
Ph. 317-261-0500
www.usalf.org

USA Track & Field is the governing body for track and field, long-distance running, and race walking in the United States. This non-profit organization's mission is to "…provide vision and leadership to the sport of track and field in the U.S. and to promote the pursuit of excellence from youth to masters, from grassroots to Olympics." USA Track & Field supports initiatives like Junior Olympics and programs that develop both male and female athletes of all ages. This is a 100,000-member association that conducts educational programs and athletic clinics nationwide.

Get Buff! BIKING In the City!

Bicycle Club of Lake County

PO Box 521
Libertyville, IL 60048
Ph. 847-604-0520
www.bikebclc.com

The Bicycle Club of Lake County (BCLC) is a cycling club that has been serving cyclists in the Northern suburbs for over 20 years. Dedicated to fun and fitness, BCLC offers numerous rides throughout the week and on weekends. Rides vary in length from 10 to 75 miles. Club members are very active in the planning of rides and activities such as regular singles rides, an annual Easter Brunch Ride, an annual riding event called the Ramble that consists of 30 to 100 mile routes, dinner and movie nights, wine tasting and ethnic dinner nights and much more. There is also a monthly newsletter called *Quick Release* that keeps members abreast of club rides, activities, and cycling information. Monthly meetings are also held to provide the latest information on cycling.

Chicago Cycling Club

PO Box 1178
Chicago, IL 60690
Ph. 773-509-8093
www.chicagocyclingclub.org

The Chicago Cycling Club offers weekday and weekend rides through Chicago Neighborhoods that range from 15 miles to 100 miles that suit riders of varying abilities. Sunday rides are usually leisurely and often have unusual themes and destinations. Saturday rides are generally longer and great for intermediate to advanced riders. For the more advanced cyclist, there is a monthly 100-mile ride. Other types of rides include training rides for cyclists training for competitions, "get acquainted rides" for those who want to socialize, the annual Ultimate Neighborhood Ride that tours 40 Chicago neighborhoods, off road trips, family rides, and overnight camping tours. Other member benefits include a monthly newsletter called *The Derailleur Mailleur*, group restaurant outings, holiday parties, membership directories, and monthly meetings.

Elmhurst Bicycle Club

P.O. Box 902
Elmhurst, IL 60126
Ph. 630-415-BIKE (2453)
www.elmhurstbicycling.org

The Elmhurst Bicycle Club serves cyclists in the Western suburbs, Northern Illinois and beyond. This active group of cyclists rides day or night all year round. Cyclists of all skill levels are welcome. Themed rides include the Halloween Costume Ride and other club activities include skiing and hiking. Club meetings give members an opportunity to socialize and to receive information on biking.

Evanston Bicycle Club

P.O. Box 1981
Evanston, IL 60204
Ph. 847-866-7743
www.evanstonbikeclub.org

The Evanston Bicycle Club organizes both recreational and competitive rides. Bicycle rides range from very short to as long as one week. Other activities include weekend camping and biking trips, ski weekends, and summer picnics. Club meetings are also held on a monthly basis.

Folks on Spokes

P.O. Box 763
Matteson, IL 60443
Ph. 708-730-5179
www.folksonspokes.com

The Folks on Spokes Bicycle Club serves the South suburbs of Chicago. Weekly rides range from 15 to 100 miles. The pace can vary from "turtle pace" where riders want to relax and enjoy the scenery, to a more aggressive speed of over 16 mph where riders can train for a race. Rides take place during the week and on weekends. There are also overnight cycle-camping trips. Meetings are held monthly with guest speakers who lead discussions on cycling topics. *The Spokin Word* newsletter informs members of events and activities taking place throughout the year. Folks on Spokes Club members are also active throughout the year, participating in non-cycling activities such as hiking and cross-country skiing, and annual parties.

Fox Valley Bicycle & Ski Club

PO Box 1073
St. Charles, IL 60174
Ph. 630-584-7353
www.fvbsc.org

The Fox Valley Bicycle & Ski Club has been appreciating the outdoors for over 30 years. Primarily serving the Fox Valley area (St.Charles, Geneva, and Aurora) the club offers regular weekly rides where the pace and distances range from easy to moderate. In addition to weekly rides, club members also enjoy socials throughout the year. The club also sponsors the Silver 60 and Swedish Days, which are two annual riding events. A club newsletter and monthly meetings keep club members informed of club news and activities.

Joliet Bicycle Club

PO Box 2758
Joliet, IL 60436
www.jolietbicycleclub.org

The Joliet Bicycle Club organizes a wide variety of rides. In fact, over 100 different rides can be found on the schedule during certain months. Five speed ranges cover levels from recreational to competitive, so cyclists of virtually any ability can join. The Joliet Bicycle Club also hosts popular invitationals such as the Sudden Century Ride, the 4th of July Ride, and the Around Illinois Back Roads ride. To spice things up, there are themed rides as well as other activities that include hiking, volleyball, roller-skating, skiing, a Christmas walk and a Chili Cook Off. Over 300 members ranging in age from 18 to 80 participate in club activities. Members also enjoy monthly meetings and a monthly club newsletter.

Naperville Bicycle Club

PO Box 3897
Naperville, IL 60567
www.napervillebikeclub.com

The Naperville Bicycle Club is dedicated to social and recreational bicycle riding. Anyone who is interested in bike riding is welcome to join. This club hosts about 10 rides per week that include easy, moderate, and fast. About 175 members enjoy other social activities in addition to bike rides. Monthly meetings give members additional opportunities to socialize.

Oak Lawn Bike Psychos

PO Box 652
Oak Lawn, IL 60454
Ph. 708-802-1804
www.bikepsychos.org

The Oak Lawn Bike Psychos is committed to promoting the sport of cycling. Based in the Southwest suburbs, this club caters to members of varying abilities. Club members enjoy weekly rides, monthly meetings, and a monthly newsletter. Monthly meeting often have guest speakers to address a variety to topics that appeal to cyclists. This club is also affiliated with associations like the League of American Bicyclists, the Chicagoland Bicycle Federation, and the Rails to Trails Conservancy.

Velo Club Roubaix, Inc

3294 Summit Ave.
Highland Park, IL 60035
Ph. 847-433-8941
www.vcrbiketeam.org

If you are an advanced cyclist, this may your dream cycling club. Velo Club Roubaix is a road cycling club that organizes rides with distances that vary from 50 to 70 miles that lasts from 2 1/2 hours to 4 hours. Speeds vary from 20 to 25 mph. Rides typically take place on weekends and weekdays. In the winter, there is a weekly ride that lasts for 2 hours followed by pizza and beer. Velo Club Roubaix has about 100 very experienced members who range in age from 20's to 50's. They are very active in road racing, mountain bike racing, cyclocross, triathlons, century rides, and weekly training rides.

Wheeling Wheelmen

P.O. Box 7304
Buffalo Grove, IL 60089
Ph. 847-520-5010
www.wheelmen.com

The Wheeling Wheelmen bicycle club began in 1970 serving those in the Northwest suburbs who enjoy road cycling as well as other activities such as mountain biking, cross country skiing, hiking, inline skating, ethnic dinners, and parties. Members stay abreast of club sponsored activities through the club hotline, newsletter or Web site. The Wheeling Wheelmen organizes nearly 300 rides during the main riding season that starts in March and ends in October. Rides are done "at your own pace". Cue sheets help riders of various abilities ride together at a comfortable speed. Distances can range from 20 miles to over 100 miles. Starting points vary as well, with most rides starting in the Northwest suburbs while some begin in Wisconsin.

Schaumburg Bicycle Club

PO Box 68353
Schaumburg, IL 60168
Ph. 847-622-5356
www.schaumburgbicycleclub.org

The Schaumburg Bicycle Club has an action-packed riding schedule. There are several rides a week, ranging in distance from 6 miles to over 20 at speeds that span 10 to 15 mph. Monthly meetings and a club newsletter keep members informed about club activities, news, and ride schedules.

Biking!
RESOURCES
In the City!

Chicago Area Mountain Bikers

PO Box 444
Oak Forest, IL 60452
Ph. 847-470-4266
www.cambr.org

If you love mountain biking and do not want to travel hundreds of miles away to enjoy the sport, this is the organization for you. Chicago Area Mountain Bikers (CAMBR) is an organization of about 400 members dedicated to promoting the sport of mountain biking. Members show their commitment to the sport by volunteering their time to prevent trail closings. Their volunteer efforts also encompass maintaining trails that are unpaved so people in the Chicago area can continue to enjoy mountain biking. CAMBR promotes awareness about safe and responsible use of trails for mountain biking.

Chicagoland Bicycle Federation

650 S. Clark St. Ste. 300
Chicago, IL 60605
Ph. 312-427-3325
www.biketraffic.org

The Chicagoland Bicycle Federation promotes bicycling as a way to stay active and keep fit. Thanks to the efforts of both staff and volunteers, many strides have been made so that biking is a more integral part of the City and surrounding areas. Chicagoland Bicycle Federation was integral in the Bike 2000 project—an effort devoted to reducing traffic jams and pollution by making the City more bike

club supplies everything you need to enjoy water sports including paddles, boats, life vests, etc. In addition to equipment, this boat club offers instruction to beginners as well as to those who are more experienced. Lincoln Park Boat Club also gives back to the Chicago community by offering kayaking instruction to kids attending summer camp and those who may be part of local boys and girls clubs.

Northwest Passage

1130 Greenleaf Ave.
Wilmette, IL 60091
Ph. 847-256-4409
www.nwpassage.com

Northwest Passage is an adventure travel company that was started by a former Peace Corps volunteer. This organization offers all types of adventure travel, like sea kayaking, dog sledding, cycling, expeditions, backpacking, and mountaineering to destinations that are both national and international. For that adventurous child or teen in your life, there are teen, youth, and family adventure programs.

Prairie State Canoeists

www.prairiestatecanoeists.org

Prairie State Canoeists is a non-profit organization that promotes canoeing, kayaking, and other water sports. Over 100 recreational and educational paddling excursions are organized every year. Most of the trips are around the Chicago area and other parts of the Midwest like Michigan, Wisconsin, and Indiana. Trips usually last a day, but some trips have lasted a week.

Winter! SPORTS *In the City!*

Chicago Friars Ski and Bike Club

www.chicagofriars.com

The Chicago Friars is a very energetic ski and bike club. Members enjoy being active all year round by going on biking trips, camping trips, canoeing and rafting trips, and ski trips. Past ski trips have included Ski Brule, Michigan, and Big Sky, Montana. All levels of skiers and bikers are welcome. Members also enjoy other non-ski and bike related activities including ethnic dinners, pub crawls, picnics, and more.

Fleetwind Ski Club

PO Box 607811
Chicago, IL 60660-7811
Ph. 630-415-3257
www.skifleetwind.com

This ski club encourages members to have fun all year round. Members enjoy Midwestern, Western, and European ski trips. In the summer, Fleetwind members enjoy pool parties, picnics, and canoe trips. Get-togethers are also organized at the Chicago Corinthian Yacht Club at Montrose Harbor. Members meet twice per month in Greek Town. Fleetwind is made up of a diverse group of people, ranging in age from 20's to 80's, whose skills vary from beginning to advanced levels.

Grand Prix Ski Club

5459 W. Wilson Ave.
Chicago, IL 60630
Ph. 773-777-8429
www.grandprixskiclub.com

Over 300 members, with an average age of 33, enjoy both national and international ski trips with the Grand Prix Ski Club. 65% of the members are single, so this may be a great club to meet someone special. Members meet twice per month during ski season and once a month during the summer at Dino's Pizzeria.

Hustlers Ski Club

P.O. Box 91896
Elk Grove Village, IL 60009
Ph. 847-289-4644
www.hustlersskiclub.com

With over 200 members, the Hustlers Ski Club is open to anyone 21 and older who enjoys skiing as well as other outdoor activities such as canoeing. The club also has a PSIA registered Ski school and a video library. Members enjoy both national and international ski trips. This group has a good mix of single and married people.

Ibex Ski & Snowboard Club

PO Box 1542
Palatine, IL 60078
Ph. 847-358-3385
www.members.aol.com/ibexskier

Members of the Ibex Ski & Snowboard club have about 170 members with a variety of interests, backgrounds, and professions. This club enjoys skiing and regular national and international ski trips. In addition to skiing, club members also enjoy volleyball, camping, biking, canoeing, hiking, golf, boating, and skydiving. Other social events include Ravinia outings, a chili cook-off, and an award ceremony.

Lake Shore Ski Club

www.lssc.org

For over 40 years, the Lake Shore Ski Club has brought together people who have a passion for skiing, athletic and social activities. Activities include both downhill and cross country skiing, biking, tennis, hiking and golf. Ski trips include excursions within the U.S., Canada, and Europe. Social activities include party cruises on Lake Michigan and an annual picnic. This 800-member organization holds club meetings twice per month.

Lincoln Park Ski Club

PO Box 146405
Chicago, IL 60614
Ph.312-337-CLUB
www.lincolnparkskiclub.org

The Lincoln Park Ski Club has been around for over 30 years and has nearly 300 members who tend to be younger. The majority of members are from the North side of Chicago with an age range of about 25 to 45. During ski season, club members meet twice per month. This club goes on both national and international ski trips. Members also participate in activities such as golf outings and beer garden socials.

Nordic Fox Ski Club

PO Box 5615
Naperville, IL 60567
www.nordicfox.org

The Nordic Fox Ski club promotes cross-country skiing and holds club meetings every month. Members also participate in other activities such as rock climbing, camping, biking, canoeing, and bowling. Social activities include picnics and holiday parties. Members also go on ski trips throughout the U.S. and Canada.

Oak Park Ski Club

P.O. Box 936
Oak Park, IL 60303
Ph.773-792-0102
www.oakparkskiclub.org

Started in 1955, the Oak Park Ski Club is an active organization that coordinates both national and international ski trips. Club members even own their own ski lodge in Boyne Falls, MI. There are approximately 400 club members, many of whom are single. The club holds regular meetings and distributes a monthly newsletter.

Over the Hill Gang

1324 Fredrickson Place
Highland Park, IL 60035
Ph. 847-831-2965
www.chicagolandothgskiclub.com

This is a great ski club for people 50+. Members of Over the Hill Gang enjoy skiing, socializing, as well as adventure travel. Other activities include monthly dinners, golf outings, bike riding, canoe trips, concerts, potlucks, hiking, sailing, and film discussions. The Chicago chapter is part of the International Over the Hill Gang organization. Members of the local chapter must first join the international chapter. The Chicago chapter has about 140 members and is made up of both singles and couples who lead very active lives.

Piccadilly Ski Club

PO Box 161
Clarendon Hills, IL 60514
Ph. 630-420-0040
www.piccadillyskiclub.com

This ski club started in 1970 and currently has over 250 active members. The goal of the organization is to provide a fun and affordable way for its members to enjoy skiing and snowboarding. Members enjoy both national and international ski trips as well as activities such as softball, annual picnics, and happy hours.

Pine Point Ski Club

1460 N. Sandburg Terrace #2411
Chicago, IL. 60610
Ph. 312-335-9394
http://members.tripod.com/ddreier

With approximately 200 members between the ages of 25 to 55, the Pine Point Ski Club offers both skiing and snowboarding. Members can also enjoy canoe trips, biking and camping trips, dinner nights, and picnics.

Skunk Hollow Ski and Snowboard Club

www.skunkhollowskiclub.com

Members of the Skunk Hollow Ski and Snowboard Club are 21 and older and enjoy a wide variety of social and sporting events. Club activities and events include hiking, whitewater rafting, dining out, camping, concerts, motorcycling, and socializing.

Winter Sports!
RESOURCES
In the City!

Chicago Metropolitan Ski Council

www.skicmsc.com

Formed in 1957, the Chicago Metropolitan Ski Council is a great resource for anyone who loves to ski (both cross-country and downhill) or snowboard. This organization supports 86 ski clubs by offering instructors clinics where ski and snowboard enthusiasts can learn to teach others to ski or snowboard. Member clubs also participate in local, national, and international races and trips. A publication called the *Midwest Skier*, keeps member-clubs up to date on activities and important news from the council, member clubs, and the ski industry. The council also has a great Web site that lists and briefly describes member ski clubs.

Chicago Sports Monster

4239 N. Western Ave.
Chicago, IL 60618
Ph. 773-866-2955
www.sportsmonster.net

Here's one of the largest and most popular sport and social clubs in the City. Chicago Sports Monster offers instruction for first timers as well as those who want to enhance their skills in sports like volleyball, tennis, and golf. I've participated in the volleyball college, and it was awesome! I hadn't played volleyball since I was 12, and by the end of the course, I became a much better player...i.e. I didn't get as many dirty looks from people when I played in a league or played with some serious sand volleyball players. Anyhow, leagues offered by Chicago Sports Monster include basketball, broomball, floor hockey, football, tennis, and kickball. Other sports and physical fitness activities include ballroom dance and bootcamp through Bulldog Bootcamp. This is also a great place to jumpstart your social life. Social Monster, the social arm of this organization, is great for meeting new people and making new friends. Each month, members of Social Monster enjoy a full calendar of events that includes happy hours, dinners, wine tastings, plays, and much more. If you want to take your athletic skills and your social life to the next level, this is the place to go.

Chicago Sport & Social Club

1516 N. Fremont
Chicago, IL 60622
Ph. 312-335-9596
www.chicagosportandsocialclub.com

If you love to participate in sports and you really want to meet other people, this is a great club to join. Best of all, membership is FREE! Chicago Sport and Social Club (CSSC) is one of the largest and most popular sport and social clubs in the Chicago area. The club's activities and outings have included tons of parties, concerts, watching Monday Night Football games at local pubs, and more. There was even one event for ladies only at a local spa that included complimentary spa treatments. CSSC also sponsors events that benefit local charities such as Children's Memorial Hospital and Make a Wish Foundation. Enough about the fun...let's talk about the games. CSSC organizes a wide variety of athletic leagues for all skill levels. If you're looking to meet people of the opposite sex, most of the leagues are co-ed and the men to women ratios tend to be 1:1. Leagues include soccer, football, floor hockey, basketball, volleyball (indoor, outdoor, and beach), softball, bowling, kickball, and tennis. Other sports include running (marathon training), dance classes, kayaking, rock climbing, and golf. This is a great place to socialize, stay fit, and have fun.

Chicago Park District

Ph. 312-742-PLAY
www.chicagoparkdistrict.com

The Chicago Park District is one of the most affordable and convenient ways to enjoy sports in Chicago. There are a wide variety of sports and leagues available to Chicago residents of all ages. Leagues include basketball, baseball, volleyball, swimming, soccer, tennis, kickboxing, and softball. Other activities include music, arts and crafts, sailing, pottery, Special Olympics, quilting, aerobics, walking, weight training, wood crafting, yoga, and writing workshops. Activities vary by park district location. For more information on the specific activities offered by each individual park district, see the Chicago Park District Web site or refer to *@ Play Magazine*, which is published once a year.

Player's Sports

3347 N. Southport
Chicago, IL 60657
Ph. 773-528-1999
www.playerssports.net

Player's Sports is a sport and social group that has been organizing sports leagues and social events for over 10 years. They also organize adventure and ski vacations. Leagues offered include softball, football, volleyball, basketball, soccer, and hockey. Social events have included Halloween parties and get togethers at local pubs. Player's Sports has also organized trips to local, national and international destinations.

Marathon Training and Other Training Groups

Bulldog Bootcamp

4305 N. Lincoln
Chicago, IL 60618
Ph. 1-866-WoofWoof
www.bulldogbootcamp.com

They do fitness the old fashioned way! with sit-ups, push-ups, pull-ups, running, and sweat. Bulldog Bootcamp's fitness programs are run military style—in a way that challenges "enlistees" both physically and mentally without breaking down their self-confidence. People who participate in these programs are continually inspired to take their fitness levels to new heights. Types of programs offered include Basic Training—a program that is geared toward beginners and meets Monday-Friday for 4 weeks. Bulldog Bootcamp is so confident in this program that they will allow you to enroll the first 3 days for FREE. After completing Basic Training, enlistees can enroll in the BOSS (Bulldog Officers School) program, which builds on the skills gained in Basic Training. Marathon training and personal training are also available. Bulldog Bootcamp has convenient locations in Chicago and the suburbs.

MaxFitness

312-327-6666
www.maxfitchicago.com

This is a fantastic marathon-training group especially for beginners. The marathon-training program meets weekly to run along the lakefront for about 26 weeks—from April to October—to do group mileage. At the beginning of the season, runners and walkers do time trials and are then placed in appropriate groups. Each group is designated a color and has a head coach available to give advice as well as to lead weekly group runs. After some weekly runs, this program has informational sessions on running and related topics such as shoe selection, hydration, stretching, etc. Weekly emails are sent with important information and announcements. There's also a hotline and a Web site where members can get their weekly running schedules and Saturday morning start times. In addition to marathon training, MaxFitness also provides triathlon and duathlon training.

Jeff Galloway Marathon Training

2800 N. Diversey
Chicago, IL 60647
Ph. 773-509-4922
www.jeffgalloway.com

This is a very popular marathon-training program in the City. The group trains from April to October for both marathons and half marathons. Runners and walkers of all levels are welcomed. They meet every Saturday morning in Lincoln Park for weekly runs. They also participate in races such as the Chicago Distance Classic, Main Course 10k and the She's Got Sole 8k in preparation for the Chicago Marathon as well as other marathons. Conferences, retreats, and running schools are also available to members of this organization.

Union Station Multiplex Marathon Training

444 W. Jackson Blvd.
Chicago, IL 60606
Ph. 312-627-0444
www.multiplexclubs.com

This health club offers a very unique and comprehensive approach to training for a marathon. In addition to coached group runs, this marathon-training group offers coached strength training, coached yoga and Pilates, coached speed work, and coached nutrition (including individual consultations with registered dieticians). This holistic approach is not only good for completing marathons, it's also good for keeping fit.

Marathon Training for a Good Cause

If you'd like to do good and keep fit, check out some of the following non-profit organizations that offer marathon-training in exchange for raising money. Each program is different, but generally speaking, participants are offered group coaching, transportation and accommodation to run or walk a marathon in an exotic location. Some programs participate in marathons in places like Hawaii, Italy, Ireland, and even Disney World. These are great opportunities to travel, support a cause you may be passionate about, and meet other people.

Joints in Motion
300 E. Wacker Dr., Ste 300
Chicago, IL 60601
Ph. 312-372-2080 ext. 12
www.arthritis.org

Train to End Stroke
www.strokeassociation.org

Team Diabetes
30 N. Michigan Ave., Suite #2015
Chicago, IL 60602
Ph. 312-346-1805
www.diabetes.org

Team in Training
100 W. Monroe, Ste. 7610
Chicago, IL 60603
Ph. 312-651-7350 ext. 240
www.teamintraining.org

Get Buff!
Triathalon Training
In the City!

Chicago Tri Club

P.O. Box 06198
Chicago, IL 60606
www.chicagotriclub.com

The Chicago Tri Club's mission is to provide an outlet for individuals who love to come together and develop their skills and build friendships with other triathletes. Skill levels within this club range from novice to Ironman veterans. Members organize activities such as group workouts, clinics, and social events. Club members also enjoy discounts at a variety of athletic stores, which can be a big help.

Together We Tri

1-866-88WETRI
www.togetherwetri.com

This triathlon-training group welcomes triathletes of all levels who have a desire to work out with and meet other people who enjoy the sport. The club meets three times a week for group runs, they also meet regularly for group swims and spinning classes. Informational clinics and seminars are also offered. Members of this organization also get together monthly for happy hours.

Tri-Masters Sports Initiative Programs

1448 E. 52nd St.
P.O. Box 172
Chicago, IL 60615
Ph. 773-995-2082
www.trimasters.org

"Tri...and you can Master anything in life" is the motto of this non-profit organization that promotes the sport of triathlon to African-American and Latino youths. Discipline and goal setting are among the many benefits youths participating in this program receive. This is a great organization to join if you love triathlons and want to make a difference in a young person's life.

Rising Phoenix Martial Arts and Fitness

3727 N. Broadway (in Quad's Gym)
Chicago, IL 60640
Ph. 773-755-KICK (5425)
www.risingphoenixchicago.com

Located in Quad's Gym on the Northside, Rising Phoenix teaches a variety of martial arts including Shaolin Kung Fu, Tai Chi, Kickboxing, and Self-defense. Other fitness focused classes available at this new martial arts school include yoga, mat pilates, Cardio Kickboxing, Fit 'N Tone and Fit 'N Flexible. There are also martial arts programs for children from the ages of 3-13 that focus on teaching self-discipline, respect, focus, confidence and self-defense.

POW! Kickboxing

950 W. Washington
Chicago, IL 60607
Ph. 312-829-7699
www.powkickboxing.com

Housed in a 7,000 square foot facility, POW! Kickboxing is perhaps one of the largest martial arts schools and fitness facilities in the City. The facility offers full-service locker rooms, a personal training studio, a boxing ring, and a lounge. Each student at this school is put on a fitness program to improve cardio, strength, and flexibility. The forms of martial arts and other combative training include KRAV MAGA (self-defense system of the Israeli Army), Gracie/Brazilian Jiu Jitsu, Kung Fu, Aikido, Judo, Karate, and more. Specialized courses include Women's Boxing, Women's self-defense, Tai Chi for Seniors, and Olympic Tae Kwon Do.

Degerberg Academy

4717 N. Lincoln Ave.
Chicago, IL 60625
Ph. 773-728-5300
www.chicagomartialartsclasses.com

Degerberg Academy teaches a wide range of martial arts forms including Karate, Boxing, Kick Boxing, Tai Chi, Aikido, Ju Jitsu, Kung Fu, the Degerberg Blend (a mixture of self-defense systems that trains students for specific situations), and more. Special seminars are offered as well as classes for children.

Enso Yoga and Martial Arts

1329 S. Michigan Ave.
Chicago, IL 60605
Ph. 312-427-3676
www.ensostudio.com

This martial arts and yoga facility is warm and family-oriented. It offers martial arts classes such as Karate, and Capoeira, an African-Brazilian form of martial arts. Yoga and pilates are also offered.

Chang's Martial Arts and Fitness Studio

1534 N. Milwaukee Ave.
Chicago, IL 60622
Ph. 773-342-6442
www.changsmartialarts.com

Chang's Martial Arts and Fitness Studio is a family-oriented martial arts studio offering training in Tae Kwon Do, Aikido, Ju Jitsu, Cardio Kickboxing, Kali, and Mat Pilates. Located in Bucktown, this studio has been serving Chicago for the past 17 years.

Special Interets

Organizations

Writers

Travelers

Publicity

Publishing

Networking

Singles

Get Connected!

Training

Songwriters

University Alumni

Public Speaking

Leagues

Get Connected! In the City

There are tons of opportunities to connect with other people in Chicago and the suburbs. However, building relationships with people—whether platonic, romantic or professional—can be tough these days, especially in a big city. The biggest advantage of living in a large metropolitan area is probably the biggest disadvantage. The fact that there are millions of people from all walks of life makes Chicago exciting. It also makes it difficult to meet and get to know people. How many times have you walked down the street almost oblivious to others coming in the opposite direction? How many times have you gone to festivals where there are large crowds, the atmosphere is cheerful, you exchange small talk with someone in line or standing next to you, but they still remain a stranger?

Most relationships are formed in smaller groups over a period of time. That's why it's easier to form relationships in college, at work, in a professional organization, or as part of an athletic league. Even though the Internet makes it easier to meet and keep in touch, it's usually in smaller groups that meet consistently where most enduring professional and personal relationships are established.

When I moved back to Chicago from London, I realized that my interests had changed and that I didn't have as much in common with many of the friends I left behind. I needed to expand my social circle and meet people whose interests were similar to mine. Expanding your professional or social network is often easier said than done. In the real world, people around you are at various stages of life. Some people are married, some are single; some have children some don't; some are retired and some are at the pinnacle of their careers; some are open to new friendships and others want to hang out with the same group of people they have for years. The important thing to remember when meeting new people is to keep an open mind. Some of your best friends could be much older than you or of a different religious or ethnic group. You may find that a common interest in wine tasting or serving the homeless is a launching pad for a fulfilling friendship. I encourage you to use this section to expand your personal and professional network.

SPECIAL INTEREST &
Professional
ORGANIZATIONS
In the City!

National Association for Investors Corporation (NAIC)

Ph.1-877-275-6242
www.better-investing.org

The NAIC is a non-profit organization that helps everyday people learn how to become successful long-term investors. This organization holds seminars, teaches classes, and hosts fairs for individual investors as well as those who are part of an investment club. There are over 400,000 individual members of this organization, many who belong to investment clubs. NAIC also produces a monthly magazine, *Better Investing,* which provides information on companies to watch, features stories on investment clubs, and provides updates on NAIC activities. This organization also produces educational materials that help investors and investment clubs make stock and mutual fund selections. There are even educational materials and programs available for children wanting to learn about the stock market. Often, individuals seeking to become a member of an investment club or wishing to start an investment club and are looking for members find prospects at NAIC conferences and seminars. See the Web site for local NAIC events.

American Association of Individual Investors (AAII)

Ph. 1-800-428-2244
www.aaii.com

This is another non-profit organization dedicated to educating people on investing and managing their money. The AAII focuses on assisting individual investors by hosting seminars and producing publications on stock and mutual fund selection, portfolio management, and retirement planning. Local chapters and sub-chapters hold regular meetings, often with nationally recognized guest speakers, on a variety of investment topics. Call or log on to the Web site to find a local chapter near you.

International Trade Club of Chicago

Ph. 312-368-9197
www.itcc.org

The International Trade Club of Chicago (ITCC) is a non-profit trade association founded in the early 1900s. Members of this organization represent a wide range of sectors including manufacturing, technology, services, educational institutions, and government agencies. The organization's purpose is to foster and expand international trade and to promote ethical international business. Benefits of membership include professional development programs, seminars, sector-focused working groups, and networking opportunities.

Professional Women's Club of Chicago

330 S. Wells St., Suite 1110
Chicago, IL 60606
Ph. 312-461-9366
www.pwcc.org

The Professional Women's Club of Chicago is an organization dedicated to promoting the professional and personal development of its members. Meetings and luncheons that feature distinguished professional women are held regularly.

Chicago Council on Foreign Relations

332 S. Michigan Ave.
Chicago, IL 60604
Ph. 312-726-3860
www.ccfr.org

With over 7,000 members, the Chicago Council on Foreign Relations is one of the largest independent, non-profit international affairs organizations in the nation. The Council provides its members and the general public a forum to discuss international events, international issues, and American foreign policy. Over 150 meetings, lectures, seminars, conferences, and special events are held every year. These events feature policy makers as well as experts within the international relations arena. In addition to lectures and seminars, the Council also offers the opportunity to speak foreign languages through Foreign Language Dinners. Languages spoken at various dinners include Chinese, French, Spanish, and German. The Council also produces various international-oriented publications, has a travel program, and offers discounts to various international organizations such as Alliance de Française, Instituto Cervantes, and the Spanish Studios. The Council has a Young Professionals group that fosters an appreciation of foreign policy and international affairs to professionals under the age of 40. The Young Professionals group holds special social events in addition to lectures.

Kiwanis International

3636 Woodview Trace
Indianapolis, IN 46268
Ph. 317-875-8755
www.kiwanis.org

Kiwanis International is an organization dedicated to serving young children and seniors in need around the world. Local Kiwanis clubs meet regularly and often bring in guest speakers. These clubs are typically made up of business professionals interested in giving back to the community. Local Kiwanis clubs can be found by using the club locator on the Kiwanis Web site.

Lions Club International

300 W. 22nd St.
Oakbrook, IL 60523
Ph. 630-571-5466
www.lionsclubs.org

The Lions Club is another global organization that helps people in need. Its mission is simple: We Serve. Lions Clubs have been tackling issues such as blindness, drug abuse, diabetes awareness, and disaster relief for over 85 years. There are over 1.4 million members that make up about 46,000 clubs in 192 countries. Major Lions Club accomplishments include collecting and distributing over 5 million pairs of eye glasses and administering over 600,000 free professional glaucoma eye screenings as part of the fight against blindness. To find a local Lions Club, log on to the Web site and search using the club locator.

Rotary International

One Rotary Center
1560 Sherman Ave.
Evanston, IL 60201
Ph. 847-866-3000
www.rotary.org

Members of Rotary International are business and professional leaders who come together to give back to the community. They provide humanitarian service, encourage high ethical standards, and build peace and goodwill worldwide. Some of the work Rotarians do include serving disabled children, promoting international understanding, delivering programs to help increase literacy, fighting poverty and hunger, and preserving the environment. Rotarians are in 166 countries with over 1.2 million members that make up 30,000 clubs. Most clubs are non-political and non-religious and are open to all cultures and races. Membership in this organization is by invitation only through local Rotary Clubs. Those interested in becoming a Rotarian should complete and send in a prospective member form for a local club to evaluate. There is a local club locater on the Web site.

Jaycees

P.O. Box 7
Tulsa, OK 74102
Ph. 1-800-JAYCEES
www.usjaycees.org

The Jaycees are made up of young adults, ages 21-39, who are dedicated to both community service and personal improvement. There are Jaycees chapters in over 100 countries and territories. Benefits of joining the Jaycees include attending special leadership training programs, developing friendships, giving back to the community, and gaining community recognition. To find a local club, visit the Web site to view club listings.

Amnesty International

Midwest Regional Office
53 E. Jackson, Ste 731
Chicago, IL 60604
Ph. 312-427-2060
www.amnestyusa.org

Amnesty International (AI) is a humanitarian organization whose members fight for human rights across the globe. This organization engages in research and takes action with the goal of preventing and/or ending violations of human rights. There are over 1.5 million members, subscribers, and supporters around the world. These AI members take actions such as writing letters to leaders of various countries to lobby for the release of those wrongly imprisoned, or to prevent or end the torture of prisoners. To find a local group, visit the AI Web site where there is a group locator.

20th Century Railroad Club

PO Box 476
Wilmette, IL 60091
Ph. 312-829-4500
www.20thcentury.org

This organization is great for anyone who loves locomotives. Since 1971, "the Century" has been offering its members a wide range of train-related activities. There are monthly meetings with presentations on various aspects of railroading. The club also organizes local and long distance vacations. Many trips take place on chartered trains that are not regularly scheduled. Members can volunteer to be bartenders, car hosts/hostesses, cooks, and waiters/waitresses on these trips.

The Chicago Urban League

4510 S. Michigan Ave.
Chicago, IL 60653
773-285-5800
www.cul-chicago.org

The Chicago Urban League (CUL) was founded in 1916 with the mission to eliminate discrimination and segregation. This organization works for equal opportunities for African-Americans, other minorities and the poor. CUL's main focus is education, economic development, and community empowerment. Members of CUL volunteer to mentor and tutor young people as well as help plan special events. CUL also has a young professional's organization called the Metro Board that helps develop young members of CUL into leaders through community service, educational programs, and networking. For more information on the Metro Board, visit their Web site at www.metropolitanboard.com.

American Marketing Association

311 S. Wacker Drive, Suite 5800
Chicago, IL 60606
Ph. 312-542-9000
www.marketingpower.com

The American Marketing Association (AMA) is one of the largest and oldest marketing organizations in the world. This organization provides information on a variety of marketing topics in the form of case studies, research, training courses and seminars. Training courses have included the AMA Marketing Bootcamp and the Marketing Research Bootcamp. There are also regular strategic marketing conferences. The AMA Chicago Chapter hosts After Hours and other events for networking. They also host career seminars and workshops as well as publish a directory of members to assist with networking.

Chicago Association of Direct Marketers

203 N.Wabash Ave., Suite 2100
Chicago, IL 60601
312-849-CADM
www.cadm.org

The Chicago Association of Direct Marketers (CADM) is a very popular professional organization in the Midwest. Membership in this organization is open to professionals in direct marketing. CADM has several special interest groups (SIGs) including B2B direct marketing, Creative Exchange (for those focused on copywriting, artwork, and graphic design), CRM (Customer Relationship Management), Database Marketing, Direct from the Heart (Volunteer/Pro Bono Work), Direct Broadcast, E-Commerce, Entrepreneur Exchange, Non-Profit Direct Marketing, Production, and Teleservices. The CADM and its SIGs offer special luncheons featuring distinguished professionals in the direct marketing industry. There are also networking and career development opportunities such as the CADM Basic Course, the annual Non-profit Direct Marketing Conference, the annual DM Days Expo and a DM competition. CADM also offers hosts the annual Tempo Awards where organizations may submit samples of their direct marketing work to be judged under several categories.

National Black MBA Association

P.O. Box 8513
Chicago, IL 60680
Ph. 312-458-9161
www.ccnbmbaa.org

The National Black MBA Association began in 1970 to promote business leadership in business and economic growth within the African-American community. Over 6,000 members nationwide and over 400 corporate partnerships make this a great networking organization for African-Americans either holding or pursuing a Masters in Business Administration. The organization offers networking functions, an annual conference, career fairs and expos, an entrepreneurs' forum, leadership seminars, scholarship opportunities business plan competitions, and much more. Members also give back to the community through programs such as Leaders of Tomorrow (LOT), a mentoring program for high school students. The Chicago chapter has over 800 members and offers an e-newsletter that updates members on upcoming events throughout the year.

National Society of Hispanic MBAs

P.O. Box 1204
Chicago, IL 60690
Ph. 312-409-5628
http://chicago.nshmba.org

Founded in 1988, the National Society of Hispanic MBAs (NSHMBA) is an organization that fosters Hispanic leadership through professional development and higher education. There are over 6,000 members nationwide within 29 chapters. Networking and professional development opportunities include an annual conference, career fairs, leadership seminars, special interest workshops, a marketing case competition, and much more.

Business Marketing Association

1920 N. Clark St. Suite 10A
Chicago, IL 60614
Ph. 312-943-8040
www.bmachicago.org

The Business Marketing Association focuses on business –to-business (B2B) marketing and communications. The group provides education, training, and professional development to B2B marketers through national and local seminars, conferences, and other programs. There are regular breakfast roundtables and luncheon seminars on various topics. The Business Marketing Association also awards excellence in B2B marketing and offers a program that certifies individuals in B2B marketing.

American Business Women's Association

Ph.1-866-281-2143
www.abwa-chicago.org

A man who saw women displaced from their jobs after men retuned home from the war started this organization in 1949. Seeing a need for leadership, training, and networking for women, he established a group that would become the 70,000+ member organization that it is today. The Chicago chapter has over 75 members and continues to grow. Monthly meetings usually held at the Columbia Yacht Club feature guest speakers who cover a variety of topics that are relevant to women in business.

Chicago Women in Publishing

P.O. Box 268107
Chicago, IL 60626
Ph. 312-641-6311
www.cwip.org

Chicago Women in Publishing (CWIP) offers educational programs, networking events, and an annual conference to help women advance their careers in publicity. The organization publishes a newsletter called *CLIPS*, a membership directory, a freelance directory, and an online job listing service called *Jobvine*.

Public Relations Society of America

1000 N. Rand Rd., Suite 214
Wauconda, IL 60084
847-526-2010
www.prsachicago.com

The purpose of the Public Relations Society of America (PRSA) is to unify, strengthen, and advance the profession of public relations. Approximately 20,000 members make up 116 chapters. The organization offers members professional development opportunities such as seminars, webinars, and teleconferences. This organization also produces two PR publications *The Strategist*, a senior level quarterly magazine, and *Public Relations Tactics*, a fun easy to read monthly tabloid written by seasoned professionals.

Publicity Club of Chicago

P.O. Box 10916
Chicago, IL 60610
Tel. 773-463-5560
www.publicity.org

The Publicity Club of Chicago began in 1941 and is one of the largest independent PR membership organizations. It offers networking and educational opportunities as well as a forum to exchange ideas and information with peers in the industry. Events include monthly luncheons with guest speakers who discuss current topics such as "Building Your Business" and "PR and the Hispanic Market".

Chicago Advertising Federation

4700 West Lake Ave.
Glenview, IL 60025
Ph. 847-375-4728
www.chicagoadfed.org

This is one of the oldest advertising organizations in Chicago. Members hold luncheons every quarter with distinguished guest speakers. There are also educational seminars for professional growth and development as well as fun social events like volleyball tournaments, bowling, and beach bashes.

Independent Writers of Chicago

PMB 119
5465 W. Grand Ave., Suite 100
Gurnee, IL 60031
Ph. 847-855-6670
www.iwoc.org

This is one of the largest organizations for freelance writers in the Midwest. It provides educational and social programs as well as networking opportunities. A directory of writers and other communications specialists is published every year.

Chicago Songwriters Collective

www.chicagosongwriters.com

The Chicago Songwriters Collective is a non-profit organization that supports songwriters. It offers opportunities for both networking and education. Membership benefits include a quarterly newsletter called *Collective Ear*, exposure to other arts organizations, and access to a network of other songwriters and musicians.

Chicago Gay & Lesbian Chamber of Commerce

1210 W. Rosedale
Chicago, IL 60660
Ph. 773-303-0167
www.GLChamber.org

This organization was founded in 1996 to support the gay, lesbian, and bisexual and transgender business community. The organization offers networking, marketing, and promotions opportunities. There are over 600 member businesses in the City and suburbs. Membership varies based on the size of the business as well as type.

Chicagoland Chamber of Commerce

One IBM Plaza
330 N. Wabash, Suite 2800
Chicago, IL 60611
Ph. 312-494-6700
www.chicagolandchamber.org

The Chicagoland Chamber of Commerce wants to make Chicago the most business friendly City in America. This chamber is focused on issues that impact businesses, including taxation, transportation, education, and small business support. The chamber holds special events such as luncheons with distinguished speakers and breakfast series that feature specific business topics. Membership benefits include insurance programs as well as discounts on cellular services. Membership varies by size and type of business.

Latin American Chamber of Commerce

3512 West Fullerton
Chicago, IL 60647
Ph. 773-252-5211
www.LACC1.com

The Latin American Chamber of Commerce was founded in 1976 by 18 small businesses. Today, over 1,000 members make it the largest Hispanic trade association in Illinois. This chamber's area of expertise includes business financing; writing loan packages and obtaining financing; procuring contracts; and business consulting.

Chicago Association of Women Business Owners

330 South Wells Street, Suite 1110
Chicago, IL 60606
Ph. 312-322-0990
www.nawbochicago.org

The Chicago Association of Women Business Owners is part of NAWBO—the National Association of Women Business Owners. This organization currently has chapters in over 80 cities. The Chicago chapter is one of the largest, offering networking, educational, advocacy, and growth opportunities. There are over 600 members and corporate partners in the Chicago Chapter. Special interest groups within the organization include Windy City Investors (an investment club) and Spouse Business Partners Group. There is also a special interest group that engages in various cultural activities in Chicago. Other activities and events include an annual holiday party, regular luncheons, and networking socials.

Chicago Professional Networking Association

P.O.Box 146368
Chicago, IL 60614
Ph. 773-296-CPNA (2762)
www.cpna.org

This association supports gays and lesbians by providing education, networking opportunities, and advocacy. Issues addressed at meetings include hate crimes, coming out at work, and voting. The organization also has social events such as "First Fridays", wine tastings, and other parties and networking events.

Association of Information Technology Professionals

P.O. Box 809189
Chicago, IL 60680-9189
Ph. 312-245-1070
www.aitpchicago.com

The Association of Information Technology Professionals (AITP) offers opportunities for leadership and education in IT. Activities include monthly dinner meetings and luncheons with local national and international IT leaders who discuss relevant IT topics. This organization also has special interest groups such as CRM, e-commerce, wireless, and more. A membership directory and a newsletter called *Shoreline* keeps members informed of events, news, and upcoming activities.

Women in Technology International

www.witi.com

This organization was founded in 1989 to help advance women in the field of technology. Its core values are "build, empower, and inspire." Members are provided with an international network that supports them through educational and leadership programs. There is also an outreach program for girls that gives members the opportunity to give back by inspiring more girls to enter the technology field. There are over 450 members in the Chicago chapter. Meetings are held once per month in both the City and suburbs.

American Association of University Women

1111 Sixteenth St. N.W.
Washington, DC 20036
Ph. 800-326-AAUW
www.aauw.org

The American Association of University Women (AAUW) is an organization that promotes education and equality for women and girls. The AAUW was founded in 1881 and has over 100,000 members within its 1300 branches. Several branches exist in the Chicagoland area. Branch activities vary by location but may include book clubs, ethnic dining, community service, and discussion groups. Local groups can be found on the AAUW Web site.

Toastmasters International

P.O. Box 9052
Mission Viejo, CA 92690
Ph. 1-800-9WE-SPEAK
www.toastmasters.org

Toastmasters International is a non-profit organization, dedicated to helping people overcome one of life's biggest fears… public speaking. This organization has over 190,000 members that make up over 9,000 clubs in 70 countries. Since its inception, Toastmasters has helped over 4 million people improve their public speaking skills. Some famous Toastmasters include author and motivational speaker Napoleon

Hill, tennis player Billie Jean King, business owner Debbie Fields Rose (Mrs. Field's Cookies) and actor Tim Allen. In a typical meeting, members deliver prepared and impromptu speeches at varying lengths and are also evaluated by fellow Toastmasters. Most clubs meet for one hour per week and groups are made up of 20-30 people. To find a club near you, use the club locator on the Toastmasters International Web site.

SOCIALIAZING, Networking & DATING *In the City!*

Highlife Adventures, Inc.

3047 N. Lincoln Ave. Suite 202
Chicago, IL 60657
Ph. 773-327-FUNN
www.highlifeadventures.com

HighLife Adventures, Inc. is a membership based social club for singles with over 2,000 members. HighLife is one of Chicago's popular social clubs for singles because of the wide variety of activities they plan. Members are mailed a calendar of events every month, which includes organized events and activities such as dining, socials, volleyball games and leagues, classes in yoga, improv, candle making, singing and more. Other activities include national and international vacations to Spain, Mexico, Colorado, New York, and Boston, speed dating parties, concerts at Ravinia, plays and musicals, comedy shows, movie nights, and game nights. There is something to do practically every day of the week with HighLife Adventures.

Chicago Social Monster/Sports Monster

4237 N. Western Ave.
Chicago, IL 60618
Ph. 773-866-2955 or 773-313-0038
www.socialmonster.com

Chicago Social Monster is the social division of Chicago Sports Monster. This club is open to both married and single people. "Social Monsters" enjoy scheduled events like movies, happy hours, theatre, and more. Social Monsters average between 23-35 years of age, and the male-female ratio is about ratio is 50/50 (for Sports Monster it's about 60/40). To offer members a wider selection of events and an opportunity to meet more people, Social Monster has partnered with Lincoln Park Young Professionals LPYP (see page 127), an organization with over 9,000 members. The Social Monster membership is accepted at LPYP events.

Midwest Adventure's Traveler's Society

P.O. Box 1189
Chicago, IL 60690-1189
www.midwestats.org

This is a social club for anyone who enjoys adventure travel, exploring, and visiting different cultures. Every month, members of the Midwest Adventure's Traveler's Society (MATS) get together to plan trips and social activities such as camping, hiking, biking, wine tasting, ethnic dinners, and more. This organization has over 180 members in the Chicago area and about 1,500 nationwide. Members are both single and married and annual membership dues are very reasonable.

First Friday's @ The Museum of Contemporary Art

220 E. Chicago Ave.
Chicago, IL 60611
Ph. 312-280-2260
www.mcachicago.org

The Museum of Contemporary Art (MCA) hosts "First Friday" events that usually last from 6pm-10pm. These after work events usually have live music, special exhibits, and performing arts. Hor d'oevres are provided by Wolfgang Puck and a cash bar is available. You must be 21 and older to attend MCA First Friday events.

Evening Associates with the Art Institute of Chicago

111 South Michigan Ave.
Chicago, IL 60603
Ph. 312-443-3600

Activities like *AfterHours* at the Art Institute are hosted by Evening Associates—the young professional members—of the Art Institute of Chicago. *AfterHours* takes place quarterly and combines an after work event with art appreciation. Each event centers around a theme highlighting a collection or an exhibit. There is usually live music, readings, gallery tours, hor d'oevres, and cocktails. Other Evening Associates activities include doing volunteer work for the Art Institute. Volunteer opportunities include assisting in children's art classes, giving tours, monitoring galleries, and greeting visitors.

Chicago Shakers Social & Adventure Club

Ph. 773-404-7067
www.chicagoshakers.com

Chicago Shakers Social and Adventure Club is an activities and social club for singles. Every month, a calendar is planned for members. All the Chicago Shakers members have to do is register and show up for the events. Examples of activities include sailing, black-tie events, wine tasting, martini parties, theatre, scuba diving, sky diving, happy hours, and travel.

Lincoln Park Young Professionals

1918 N. Cleveland Suite D
Chicago, IL 60614
Ph. 312-642-5097
www.lp-yp.com

Lincoln Park Young Professionals is a growing social group that currently has over 9,000 members. Founded in 1995, the group hosts parties and events at distinctive venues around the City like the Chicago Yacht Club and the Field Museum. Membership in this organization is very reasonable and is popular because members benefit from special invitations and reservations to some of the City's hottest events. They also receive special offers at various restaurants, theatres, and cultural institutions.

Willow Creek Church Young Adult Ministry and Single Adult Ministry

67 E. Algonquin Rd.
South Barrington, IL 60010
Ph. 224-512-2088
www.willowcreek.org

The Willow Creek Single Adult Ministry (SAM) and Young Adult Ministry—part of Willow Creek Church in South Barrington—are great places to meet people, make friends, and perhaps find your soul mate. SAM at Willow Creek is broken out by age group. Each age group has its own meetings, and in some cases, its own church services. Groups include *Thirty*, which caters to those between the ages of 30-35, *The Edge*—for those between the ages of 35-45, and *New Horizons*—for those 45 and older. *Single Parents* caters to single parents of all ages. There's even a ministry for children of single parents called *Champions*, which meets at the same time as *Single Parents*. Popular activities among these groups include things like Caroling at the Zoo (around Christmas time), New Year's Eve parties, Christmas parties, potlucks, and more. For active singles of all ages, there is a travel and tours group that goes to places like Spain, San Francisco, and Yosemite Park, and other fun and exotic destinations.

Willow Creek's Young Adult Ministry caters to both single and married adults from ages 18 through 20 somethings. Young adults in their early thirties also participate. This group, called *Axis*, has its own church services, social events and sports leagues. They also show their dedication to improving communities, both locally and nationally by participating in projects like building homes for *Habitat for Humanity*.

Big Ten Chicago

www.bigtenchicago.com

This organization serves as Chicago's gateway for big ten university alumni relations, events and news in and around Chicago. The website provides information all in one location for alums. Big Ten Chicago also sponsors events such as wine tasting, TV game nights (where alumni go to local bars to watch their universities play football or basketball games), Speed Dating and more, that help people keep in touch or meet for the first time. There's also information on fraternity and sorority chapters.

The Discovery Center

2940 N. Lincoln Ave.
Chicago, IL 60657
Ph. 773-348-8120
www.discoverycenter.cc

Both singles and couples take classes at The Discovery Center, but it's really great for singles. It's a great for singles, not only because of its fun and interesting classes, but also because it offers classes, seminars, and socials with the single person in mind. For example, relationship experts teach classes like Street Flirting, How to Talk to Anyone Anytime, Mastering the Art of Dating & Mingling, and much more. While you're at it, you can also take other classes that interest you like ice-skating, pottery, ballet, and business and career classes.

SINGLES CLUBS *Dining* *In the City!*

Single Gourmet

29020 W. Grand Ave., Suite 100
Chicago, IL 60622
Ph. 773-772-3535
www.singlegourmetchicago.com

Single Gourmet arranges dinner parties and other social events. With over 1,200 members, Single Gourmet club members enjoy dinner parties at hot spots like Greek Islands, Fortunato, Chop House, Carlucci, and Bahama Breeze. Members also enjoy other events like cruises, wine tastings, and sporting events. Trips include Cubs and Sox spring training in Arizona, a Mexican Riviera cruise, and more. Club membership fees are very reasonable.

8 at 8 Dinner Club

P.O. Box 147251
Chicago, IL 60614
Ph. 312-583-0888
www.8at8.com

This dining club arranges dinner parties for four single women and 4 single men at upscale Chicagoland restaurants. The 8 at 8 staff matches people for dinner parties based on their interests and backgrounds. In addition to dinner parties, this club organizes events like beer and wine tastings, dinner theatre outings, holiday parties, and scavenger hunts.

Gourmet Advocates/Club Suburbia

1414 W. Byron St., Suite 2E
Chicago, IL 60613
www.gourmetadvocates.com
Ph.773-929-6534

Gourmet Advocates is a dining and social club for singles between the ages of 30 and 50. This club arranges dinners and other socials every month at Chicago area hot spots. Sample events include a New Year's Eve party at *Gibson's Steakhouse*, Lakeview Latin Tasting @ *Cabo Grill* & *La Taverna Tapatia*, Italian cuisine and piano favorites at *Cuccina Roma*, and more. Other social events include wine tastings, after work mixers, and black tie events. Gourmet Advocates also keeps its members informed through an e-newsletter called *Gourmet for Today!*, which includes recipes, restaurant and wine reviews, articles on singles—related topics, and information on upcoming events.

Do Good!

Be a Greeter

Volunteer

Sign Up

Feel Good

Research

Be a Host

Help a Kid

Donate

Training

Fundraising

Teaching

Make a Difference

Be a Coach

Do Good! In the City

Chicago has countless opportunities for anyone looking to make a difference in someone's life. We've all got something we can share with someone else—whether it's helping a fifth grader do her math homework, teaching a first grader how to play golf, planting a tree, painting a house, or bringing food to someone who is elderly. Doing volunteer work not only allows you to make a difference, it also allows you to learn new skills and discover new talents. Never in a million years would I have thought I'd enjoy painting, had I not participated in a volunteer project with Chicago Cares where I helped to paint a swing set and a sliding board in one of Chicago's parks. Not only did I enjoy it, I found that I was pretty good at it. When choosing an organization, I encourage you to not only to do what you love, but to also try something you wouldn't ordinarily. You'll develop new skills and discover new passions.

Charities

20/30 Club

858 W. Armitage, Suite 175
Chicago, IL 60614
Ph. 312-409-3454
www.2030club.org

The 20/30 Club is a group of young Chicago men that works with local children's charities that serve Chicago's needy children. Charities that 20/30 club members work with include Mercy Home for Boys, One Step at a Time, Youth Outreach Services, Teen Living, and Kaleidoscope. Volunteer opportunities include participating in the Hoops to Homework program where club members first help kids with their homework and afterwards with their jump shots. 20/30 club members also organize and attend fun social events like the Casino Swing and the Moonlight Cruise, which raise money to support local charities.

American Cancer Society

77 E. Monroe, 12th Floor
Chicago, IL 60603
Ph. 312-372-0471
www.cancer.org

If you want to make a difference in the fight against cancer, consider the American Cancer Society (ACS). ACS strives to prevent and ultimately eliminate cancer through research, education, advocacy, and service. This organization has over 3,400 local offices around the country, including several in the Chicagoland area. Volunteer opportunities include fundraising, educating the public on cancer prevention and detection, letter writing to Congress for improved legislation, and more.

American Diabetes Association

30 N. Michigan Ave., Suite 2015
Chicago, IL 60602
Ph. 312-346-1805
www.diabetes.org

The battle against diabetes needs soldiers and here's the place to enlist. This disease kills millions every year, but doesn't have to. The American Diabetes Association is a national organization that provides information, conducts research, and engages in advocacy to achieve its goal of preventing and finding a cure for diabetes. A really fun way to get involved while keeping fit is by participating in programs like Team Diabetes (or Team D). Team D is a marathon-training program where participants raise funds to support the organization in exchange for being professionally trained to run or walk a full or half marathon. Other distances are also available. In addition to training, entry into the race, travel, and accommodations are also provided. The required amount of money participants need to raise depends on the location of the race. Races are held all over the world at destinations like Rome, Hawaii, and Disney World.

Art Institute of Chicago

111 S. Michigan Ave.
Chicago, IL 60603
Ph. 312-443-3600
www.artic.edu

The Art Institute of Chicago is one of the City's premier art museums, which makes it a very interesting place to volunteer, especially if you have a passion for art. Volunteer opportunities include greeting museum visitors, giving directions throughout the museum, and assisting guests with membership registration and renewal. Other opportunities include behind the scenes work like conducting research, translating documents, data entry, and other administrative tasks. The Art Institute also looks for volunteers to be hosts or hostesses at jazz nights, poetry readings, and special exhibits.

Aunt Martha's Youth Centers

233 W. Joe Orr Rd., North Bldg
Chicago Heights, IL 60411
Ph. 708-754-1044
www.auntmarthas.org

Aunt Martha's is a private, non-profit organization that supports children, youth, and families in need by providing services and shelter. This is truly a remarkable agency for young people and families. Several years ago, I volunteered at a one of the group homes for children. Most of those kids had experienced more in life as children than I had as an adult. Their overall ability to be happy truly inspired me. Volunteer opportunities at Aunt Martha's include mentoring, supervising group activities, and performing administrative tasks.

Big Brother/Big Sister

28 E. Jackson St., Suite 1800
Chicago, IL 60604
Ph. 312-427-0637
www.bbbschgo.org

If you've always wanted a little brother or a little sister, consider this organization. For nearly 100 years, Big Brother/Big Sister has been a leader in developing mentoring relationships between adults and youth. Types of activities that "Bigs and Littles" participate in include sports, watching movies, cooking, doing homework, visiting museums, taking walks, and doing volunteer work together. This is a great organization for those who love working closely with children.

Bottomless Closet

445 N. Wells, Suite 301
Chicago, IL 60601
Ph. 312-527-9664
www.bottomlesscloset.org

If you have a passion for fashion, retail, or public speaking, this is a great organization to consider. Bottomless Closet provides clothing, employment, training, and career coaching to women on public assistance or who are part of the working poor. The goal is to empower these women with the knowledge and confidence to make a positive difference in their own lives, while making a positive difference at their new place of employment. There are a wide variety of volunteer opportunities at Bottomless Closet including, assisting with resume writing, interview preparation, development of communication skills, professional development, and image development. Other volunteer opportunities include being a personal shopper—helping clients select interview appropriate clothing from the boutique, clothing in take, inventory management, database management, assisting with mass mailings, and administrative duties.

Brookfield Zoo

3300 Golf Rd.
Brookfield, IL 60513
Ph. 708-485-0263
www.brookfieldzoo.org

Brookfield Zoo is a fun place to for animal lovers to visit and to volunteer. Volunteer opportunities include welcoming guests into the zoo, working with young kids in the Children's Zoo by narrating cow and goat milking demonstrations, telling stories, and helping young visitors make connections with the animals. Other opportunities include serving as a teacher's assistant in the zoo's formal classroom programs and leading fun activities such as arts and crafts. There are also opportunities to become docents—a volunteer position that requires extensive training provided by the zoo. Docents narrate zoo exhibits and provide educational presentations for some of the zoo's special events.

Cabrini Green Tutoring Program, Inc.

1515 N. Halsted St.
Chicago, IL 60622
Ph. 312-397-9119
www.cabrinigreentutoring.org

The Cabrini Green Tutoring Program has been around for about 36 years providing after school tutoring for kids living in the Cabrini Green neighborhood. Over 200 students in grades 1 through 6 are in the program. Volunteers help students with their homework and work with them to improve academic skills for 1.5 hours one night per week.

Chicago Abused Women's Coalition

P.O. Box 477916
Chicago, IL 60647
Ph. 773-278-4110
www.cawc.org

The Chicago Abused Women's Coalition is dedicated to ending violence against women by empowering them to help themselves and their children. Volunteers can answer hotline calls, supervise children's playgroups, and participate in special fundraising events such as an annual walk-a-thon and the annual Visions of Chocolate Gala.

Chicago Architecture Foundation

224 S. Michigan Ave.
Chicago, IL 60604
Ph. 312-922-3432
www.architecture.org

If you have a passion for architecture, and want to share your knowledge with others, a unique opportunity as a docent may exist for you at the Chicago Architecture Foundation (CAF). Docents interpret and discuss Chicago Architecture on tours that they give downtown and in surrounding Chicago neighborhoods. Training for this particular volunteer position requires taking an 11-week training program that is comparable to a graduate level course. An application and an interview with current CAF docents are required for acceptance into the program. Other opportunities to contribute to this organization include greeting guests as they visit the Chicago Architecture Foundation and administrative duties such as answering phones.

Chicago Cares

300 W. Adams, Suite 300
Chicago, IL 60006
Ph. 312-780-0800
www.chicagocares.org

This is one of the most fun and interesting volunteer organizations in the City. Chicago Cares, a part of City Cares makes volunteering for young, busy professionals easier and more convenient. Chicago Cares organizes approximately 100 group volunteer projects per month. Volunteers can choose projects from a variety of categories including working with children, adults, seniors, the environment and the homeless. If you haven't quite found your niche or passion, you can volunteer for several projects in a variety of categories. In fact, there's usually a group that commits to volunteering for at least one volunteer project in every category over a period of time. Calendars describing both long and short-term projects are mailed monthly to volunteers. Many projects last for a few hours while some meet once per week throughout the year. If you're looking for more of a leadership role, there are opportunities to become team coordinators.

Chicago Food Depository

4100 W. Ann Lurie Place
Chicago, IL 60632
Ph. 773-247-3663
www.chicagosfoodbank.org

The Chicago Food Depository is a non-profit organization that distributes food to the hungry living in Cook County. This organization works with agencies such as soup kitchens, shelters, and pantries to distribute food that is either purchased or donated. The Chicago Food Depository works with agencies such as the Inspiration Café and the Living Room Café. Volunteer Opportunities include loading food into vehicles for distribution, repackaging food, putting together care packages, holding food drives to benefit the organization, and donating food or money.

Chicago Greeters

Chicago Office of Tourism
78 East Washington Street
Chicago, IL 60602
Ph. 312-742-1190
www.chicagogreeter.com

This is the opportunity of a lifetime for anyone who loves Chicago and wants to show newcomers around. This fairly new program, designed to welcome and introduce visitors to the City, matches volunteers with visitors according to their mutual interests. Greeters lead visitors on neighborhood and themed tours such as African-American Heritage, the Lakefront, churches, Maxwell Street Market, public art, theatre, Navy Pier, and architecture. Becoming a Chicago Greeter offers the unique opportunity to meet people from different parts of the United States and from all over the world.

Chicago Park Districts

Ph. 312-742-PLAY
www.chicagoparks.com

The City of Chicago has hundreds of beautiful parks offering countless ways to give. You can help beautify the parks themselves, or serve local residents living in the park districts. Volunteer opportunities in your local or favorite park district include gardening, helping children with arts and crafts or homework in an after school program, assisting with special events such as Halloween or Christmas parties, helping with sporting events like volleyball or basketball tournaments, and greeting park visitors at special exhibits.

Chicago Youth Centers

104 S. Michigan Ave.
Chicago, IL 60603
Ph. 312-795-3500
www.chicagoyouthcenters.org

Chicago Youth Centers (CYC) is the largest independent youth services agency based in Chicago. Founded in 1956, this organization serves inner city youth through programs that focus on Nature & Environment, Math & Science, Health & Physical Development, Academic Support and Enhancement, Career Exploration/Business & Community Outreach, Leadership Development and The Arts. Volunteer opportunities include becoming a tutor or mentor; becoming a club leader, which involves providing instruction on computers, sports, and workshops on social issues; and assisting with special events such as parties and field trips. Behind the scenes opportunities include fundraising, administrative support, and repairs and maintenance.

Cystic Fibrosis Foundation

www.cff.org

The Cystic Fibrosis Foundation (CFF) is dedicated to finding a cure and helping to improve the quality of life for those living with the disease. CFF serves as a resource of information about the disease that affects thousands. Opportunities to serve this organization include participating in the Great Strides Walk-a-Thon, golf tournaments, special galas, and singles events designed to raise money and awareness about the organization and the disease. See Web site for a CFF chapter or care center near you.

Earthwatch

Ph. 630-369-5186
http://earthwatch.chicago.home.att.net/

The mission of the Earthwatch Institute is, "…to promote the sustainable conservation of our natural resources and cultural heritage by creating partnerships among scientists, the general public, education, and business." This organization is a non-profit international organization with 30,000 members and supporters worldwide. 3,500 volunteer members work with 120 research scientists every year on field research projects around the world. Earthwatch Chicago supports the Earthwatch Institute. Throughout the year, Earthwatch Chicago hosts Poster Brunches where volunteers share their experiences display photos from their expeditions to places such as Africa, Australia, and the UK. These brunches educate and inspire others to volunteer for future field projects.

Friends of the Parks

55 E. Washington St., Suite 1911
Chicago, IL 60602
Ph. 312-857-2757
www.fotp.org

Friends of the Parks works to protect, preserve, and improve Chicago's parks. This organization was formed in 1975 to help ensure that tax dollars were spent wisely on the upkeep of parks and public spaces in Chicago. Volunteer opportunities include becoming a Volunteer in Parks (VIP), which is a group of volunteers dedicated to park clean-ups, beautification, and related projects. Each year, the VIPs organize 10,000 people to participate in park beautification throughout the City. Other volunteer opportunities include adopting a park or a beach and assisting with the organization and coordination of community service projects in the parks for groups like businesses or universities that encourage environmental giving or want to use the activity for team building.

Fairy Godmother Foundation

2020 Lincoln Park West Suite 37E
Chicago, IL 60614
Ph. 773-388-1160
www.fairygodmother.org

The Fairy Godmother Foundation makes wishes come true for individuals (over 18 years of age) who have terminal illnesses. The average wish recipient is a 40-year-old mother who wants to take her children to Disney World before she dies. Volunteer opportunities include assisting in the wish fulfillment by doing things like meeting families at airports or on some portion of their dream vacation. Other opportunities include donating money, airline miles, airline tickets, and timeshare weeks. Volunteers also help find individuals or companies to sponsor a wish; write and edit newsletters; write press releases; and perform administrative duties.

Field Museum

1400 S. Lake Shore Dr.
Chicago, IL 60605
Ph. 312-922-9410
www.fmnh.org

The Field Museum is a great place to volunteer if you love nature, cultures, and the history of the two. The Field Museum has been home to special exhibits like Sue (the dinosaur). Volunteer opportunities at the Field Museum include working on small construction projects within the museum, becoming a facilitator for special exhibits and welcoming visitors into the museum. Volunteers are also needed to perform clerical duties like data entry and answering phones.

Gallery 37

66 E. Randolph St.
Chicago, IL 60601
Ph. 312-744-8925
www.gallery37.org

Gallery 37 is a program sponsored by the City of Chicago that provides young people with quality education and job training in the field of art. This program serves Chicago youth regardless of gender, race, economic background or physical ability. Through this program, young people are given an opportunity to work with an artist to sharpen their creative skills. Volunteers can become a mentor, support Gallery 37 special events and festivals, serve as classroom assistants, collect information about internship and study abroad opportunities for youth in the program, and become a docent or tour guide of the CenterSpace Gallery where artwork is displayed.

Garfield Park Conservatory

300 N. Central Park Ave.
Chicago, IL 60624
Ph. 773-638-1776 ext. 20
www.garfieldconservatory.org

For all you green thumbs, this is the volunteer opportunity from heaven—well actually earth ☺. Located on Chicago's West Side in Garfield Park—a 185-acre site—Garfield Park Conservatory is one of the largest and most beautiful conservatories in the U.S. The Conservatory covers 4.5 acres inside and out. This historical landmark began undergoing major renovations starting in 1994. Today, as a part of the improvements, there is now a Demonstration Garden that offers local gardeners and garden clubs, environmentalists, and other interested local residents an opportunity to learn and to teach gardening techniques that are specific to growing and maintaining a garden in an urban area. Volunteer opportunities include assisting with building renovations, leading children's classes in gardening, exploring plant life, and arts and crafts. Other opportunities include becoming a tour guide and providing visitors with information about the conservatory.

Girl Scouts

420 5th Ave.
New York, NY 10018
Ph. 1-800-478-7248
www.girlscouts.org

Green and white uniforms, cookies, and camping are what usually come to mind when most people think of Girl Scouts. Girl Scouts still sell cookies, go camping and wear green and white, however, this organization does a lot more to meet the needs of today's girl. Contemporary programs like *Trippers*, allow girls who are not part of a troop to participate in girl scouting by periodically going on field trips. There are also programs that address modern-day challenges such as self-esteem and peer pressure. This organization has also developed educational programs that encourage girls to embrace technology and perhaps consider a career in a high tech field. Girl Scouts is the leading organization dedicated solely to the growth and development of "every girl everywhere. "Adult Leaders pass on values, social conscience, and strong character to the girls they serve. Volunteers serve on council boards (opportunity open to both men and women), lead troops, become mentors, and chaperone day trips. See the Web site to locate a council near you.

HighSight

1107 N. Orleans
Chicago, IL 60601
Ph. 312-787-9824
www.highsight.org

HighSight is a non-profit organization that helps inner city high school kids enter and excel in the private school of their choice. There are currently over 100 students enrolled in 24 schools. Each of these students receives financial, academic, and social support through HighSight. Volunteer opportunities include mentoring and tutoring students, as well as organizing fundraisers.

Inner City Teaching Corps

3141 W. Jackson
Chicago, IL 60612
Ph. 773-265-7240
www.ictc-chicago.org

This organization serves inner city youth by attracting motivated young women and men to serve as teachers. Those who serve children through Inner City Teaching Corps inspire students to be their best. Volunteer opportunities with this organization include becoming a teacher in an inner city parochial school that serves low-income children and organizing fundraising events.

Inspiration Café/Inspiration Corporation

4554 N. Broadway, Suite 207
Chicago, IL 60640
Ph. 773-878-0981
www.inspirationcorp.org

Not only does this organization serve food to the homeless, it serves up hope and inspiration. Inspiration Café is a non-profit organization that provides services to the homeless that are designed to help them get back on the road to independence with dignity and respect. The café looks a lot like an upscale restaurant. Volunteers wait on all guests providing personalized service and respect. Food is freshly prepared from menus provided. In addition to the homeless, the Inspiration Café serves the underemployed, mentally ill, socially isolated, and recovering substance abusers. The Café also offers job training. Volunteer opportunities include cooking, serving meals, and creating bag lunches. Other opportunities include facilitating computer classes and conducting job training classes on topics like resume writing and interviewing skills. There are also administrative and clerical opportunities. Another way to support this organization is by taking cooking classes. If you enjoy cooking, Inspiration Café offers some of the most affordable cooking classes in the City led by well-known chefs. 100% of the proceeds benefit the Café.

Jr. League of Chicago

1447 N. Astor St.
Chicago, IL 60610
Ph. 312-664-4462
www.jlchi.org

The Jr. League of Chicago is an organization of women committed to promoting volunteerism and improving the community. This organization reaches out to women of all races and religions who demonstrate an interest in and a commitment to volunteerism. New members go through one year of training and the training process continues after this period. The Jr. League is a membership-based organization with over 2,400 members. Volunteer opportunities exist in the areas of mentoring, advocacy, and education.

Juvenile Diabetes Research Foundation Illinois

500 N. Dearborn St. Suite 305
Chicago, IL 60610
312-670-0313
www.jdrfillinois.org

The Juvenile Diabetes Research Foundation (JDRF) is dedicated to finding a cure for diabetes and its complications through support of research. Founded in the 1970's by concerned parents of children with type-1 diabetes, JDRF is the leading non-profit organization that funds type-1 diabetes research worldwide. Thus far, JDRF has awarded $600 million to diabetes research. Volunteer opportunities include working at fundraising events, helping to set up walk sites, and coordinating silent auctions on gala nights. Individuals can also serve on committees and develop communications strategies, assist with corporate recruitment, or help coordinate walk-a-thons. Other opportunities include becoming an advocate and contacting elected officials about diabetes-related issues.

Lambs Farm

14245 W. Rockland Rd.
Libertyville, IL 60048
Ph. 847-362-4636
www.lambsfarm.com

Lambs Farm's mission is to empower people with developmental disabilities to lead personally fulfilling lives. It does this through serving its clients in group homes that focus on independent living. This organization offers occupational programs that help the people they serve develop work place skills. It also provides social and recreational opportunities like theatre, sports, Special Olympics and music. Volunteer opportunities include instructing classes in arts and crafts; assisting with social events by acting as Santa Claus and Easter Bunny helpers; assisting in the Lambs Farm restaurant; doing grounds work, performing administrative and clerical duties; taking pictures, and much more.

Lincoln Park Zoo

2200 N. Cannon Dr.
Chicago, IL 60614
Ph. 312-742-2124
www.lpzoo.com

Lincoln Park Zoo is one of the oldest zoos in the country and is the only free cultural institution in Chicago. If you love nature, kids, and animals, then this is a great place to volunteer. One volunteer opportunity at Lincoln Park Zoo is to become a docent. Docents are specially trained volunteers who lead tours, teach classes, interpret exhibits and education stations, handle small animals, assist with activities in the children's zoo, and visit schools. These volunteers commit 4 hours per week for one year. Lincoln Park Zoo offers other volunteer opportunities in gardening and guest services. Volunteers can also assist with special events and projects like helping to coordinate the annual Zoo Lights Festival.

Little City Foundation

1760 W. Algonquin Rd.
Palatine, IL 60067
Ph. 847-358-5510
www.littlecity.org

The Little City Foundation provides services to help children and adults challenged with mental retardation or other developmental disabilities lead meaningful, productive, and dignified lives. For adults, this organization offers suitable living arrangements, teaches job skills, and assists with job placements. For children, the Little City Foundation offers adoption and foster care services. Volunteer opportunities include providing companionship to Little City Foundation clients; assisting with arts & crafts, sports & fitness and other recreational activities; providing office support and assisting with special events and fundraising. The Little City Foundation also runs a resale shop called Frontporch that needs assistance with sales, stocking, mending donated items, and procuring donations.

Lydia Home

4300 W. Irving Park Rd.
Chicago, IL 60641
Ph. 773-736-1447

The Lydia Home is a national organization whose mission is to strengthen families and to care for children when their families cannot. This organization, which is headquartered in Chicago, has been around for over 85 years. It runs a residential treatment program for kids, a pre-school, and a counseling center. The Lydia Home has a variety of programs including Foster Care, Healthy Families, Mothers Program, Safe Families, and Abstinence Education. The Lydia Home is now international, partnering with agencies that serve children living in countries like Jamaica, India, China, South Africa and Romania. Volunteer opportunities include mentoring and foster parenting. You can also make a difference by either making or procuring donations of "in-kind" gifts like school uniforms, underwear, roller skates, gift certificates, and large vans.

Lynn Sage Cancer Research Foundation

750 North Lake Shore Dr., Suite 542
Chicago, IL 60611
Ph. 312-926-0439
www.lynnsage.org

The Lynn Sage Foundation was established in 1985 in honor of Lynn Sage who died from breast cancer in her early thirties. The organization supports patient care, outreach programs, and breast cancer research. In 1991, the foundation formed a partnership with Northwestern University Hospital to provide women who have breast cancer with the best care and support. Volunteers are always needed to help organize and support fundraising events.

March of Dimes

111 W. Jackson, 22nd Floor
Chicago, IL 60604
Ph. 312-435-4007
www.marchofdimesillinois.org

The March of Dimes was founded to help prevent birth defects and infant mortality. This organization funds research programs, community services, advocacy and education to save babies.

Do Good! In the City

Volunteers can become a committee member for a special event; serve on a sub-committee focused on sales and sponsorships; donate or recruit businesses to donate "in kind" services; donate or solicit businesses to donate items for auctions or sweepstakes; publicize events and educational campaigns; make presentations to companies, schools, and clubs; and assist in the distribution of information at health fairs. Other opportunities include participating in the annual WalkAmerica walk-a-thon either as a walker or a team coordinator.

Museum of Science & Industry

57th St. and Lake Shore Dr.
Chicago, IL 60603
Ph. 773-684-1414
www.msichicago.org

The Museum of Science and Industry first opened in the early 1930's and it was the first museum in the country to house interactive exhibits. It's also the largest science museum in the country under a single roof. The Museum of Science and Industry offers a wide variety of volunteer opportunities such as facilitating permanent and temporary exhibits; assisting guests with hands on activities; helping visitors find exhibits and recommending exhibits to visitors. Volunteers also assist in the retail store, member services, and in museum offices.

Off the Street Club

25 N. Karlov
Chicago, IL 60624
Ph. 773-533-3253
www.otsc.org

Founded in 1900, this organization is the oldest boys and girls club
in the Chicagoland area. It serves over 3,000 children from ages 14-
19 in the Garfield Park neighborhood. Off the Street Club is a safe
haven from drugs and gangs. Children served by this organization
have the opportunity to participate in arts & crafts, sports, computer
games, photography, board games, field trips, cooking, theatre, and
much more. Volunteers can become a part of "Third Thursday at
the Club" and spend an evening with a child engaged in an activity
such as playing chess or basketball. There is also a program called
"New Horizons" where volunteers plan and lead field trips or share
career experiences. During the summer, volunteers serve as camp
counselors. If you love to cook or take pictures, the Kitchen Club and
the Photography Club are always looking for volunteers. Also, for
those born to be on stage, there are music and drama programs that
need volunteers.

PAWS Chicago

3516 W. 26th St.
Chicago, IL 60623
Ph. 773-935-PAWS or 773-521-1408 ext. 1
www.pawschicago.org

PAWS Chicago (which stands for Pets Are Worth Saving), is a no-
kill adoption agency that is working hard to make Chicago no-kill
City for animals without homes. Volunteer opportunities with PAWS
Chicago include feeding and playing with cats and dogs; helping out
with adoptions; cleaning kennels; and becoming foster parents for

pets until permanent homes are found. Other ways to help include answering phones in the offices, data entry, and assembling adoption packets.

Prevent Blindness

500 East Remington Road
Schaumburg, IL 60173
Ph. 847-843-2020
www.preventblindness.org/il

Prevent Blindness America is our country's leading volunteer organization dedicated to fighting and preventing blindness. This organization fulfills its mission through education, vision screening training, research, and patient and community service programs.

Opportunities to help prevent blindness include helping to screen pre-school aged children and adults to detect eye problems that can lead to blindness; planning special events to raise money and/or awareness; promoting eye health and safety in your local community; making donations; and shopping online at the Shopping Village—the organization's online store where 5% of the value of your purchases automatically goes to Prevent Blindness America—see www.preventblindness.org for details.

Ronald McDonald House

One Kroc Dr.
Oak Brook, IL 60523
Ph. 630-623-7048
www.rmhc.com

The Ronald McDonald House is known for improving lives of the children it serves through various programs like the Ronald McDonald Care Mobiles, where free, high quality medical and dental care are brought directly to underserved children. The Ronald McDonald House also supports a program called "Changing the Face of the World" where almost $2 million in grants have been awarded to children and young adults in need of reconstructive surgery. There are over 25,000 Ronald McDonald House volunteers nationwide. Volunteer opportunities include assisting with fundraising, planning special events, and cooking meals for the children and their families. Monetary donations as well as the donation of services are always welcomed.

Shedd Aquarium

1200 S. Lake Shore Dr.
Chicago, IL 60605
Ph. 312-692-3309
www.sheddnet.org

The Shedd Aquarium promotes the appreciation of aquatic life. It's one of the largest indoor aquariums in the world, and is considered to be one of the most interesting cultural attractions in the City. This popular aquarium houses over 6,000 fishes, reptiles, amphibians, mammals, and invertebrates of approximately 750 different species. If you love the underwater life this would be a great place to volunteer. Volunteer opportunities include assisting Shedd Aquarium by teaching classes to school children; helping to maintain the animal husbandry areas, helping visitors learn about marine life, and more.

Starlight Children's Foundation

30 E. Adams, Suite 1020
Chicago, IL 60603
Ph. 312-251-7827
www.starlightmidwest.org

The Starlight Children's Foundation began in 1983 by actress Emma Sams and her cousin, producer Peter Samuelson. Emma became friends with a young cancer patient and granted him a wish of visiting Disneyland before he died. Emma and Peter were so touched by the impact the Disneyland experience had on the little boy and his mother that they formed the Starlight Children's Foundation to grant wishes to children in similar circumstances. This Los Angeles-based organization now has 13 chapters worldwide. It serves over 100,000 children every month through both in-patient and out-patient programs. Opportunities to help include coordinating special events; participating in granting a wish; fundraising; and performing office or administrative duties. Volunteers attend a one-hour orientation session to become more familiar with the organization. Once accepted into the program, training is provided to prepare volunteers for their positions.

The Cradle

2049 Ridge Ave.
Evanston, IL 60201
Ph. 847-475-5800
www.cradle.org

This adoption agency provides education and support to adults to help make good parenting decisions. This agency is one of the only adoption agencies that has a nursery on its premises that allows volunteers to hold and comfort the babies. Other volunteer opportunities include being an adoption education speaker;

performing clerical or administrative duties; being a driver; and assisting with special fundraising events such as The Cradle Ball.

The Gus Foundation

833 W. Wrightwood Ave.
Chicago, IL 60614
Ph. 773-281-5560
ww.gusfoundation.org

The Gus Foundation was established in 1995 in memory of Gus Evangelides, a toddler who died of a brain tumor. This foundation partners with Children's Memorial Hospital of Chicago to give hope to children with this disease. It raises money for research and helps children with brain tumors have access to the best possible treatments. In the year 2000, the Young Associates Board, a subset of the foundation, was established. Made up of professionals in their 20's and 30's, this board helps to provide relief to the children and their families by organizing parties at the hospital or special outings like Cubs games. This group also organizes fundraising events like the *Run for Gus* race. Volunteer opportunities with this foundation— including the Young Associates Board—are numerous and include participating in and/or organizing events like golf tournaments; restaurant openings or bar nights; stuffing newsletters; and much more.

Today's Chicago Woman Foundation

150 E. Huron St., Suite 1225
Chicago, IL 60611
Ph. 312-954-7600
www.todayschicagowoman.com

Today's Chicago Woman's Foundation (TCWF) is an organization that supports women and children in crisis situations such as domestic violence. TCWF does this by funding local organizations and projects that serve women and children who find themselves in difficult situations. Opportunities to help include attending fundraisers and social functions; serving on a committee; making monetary or in-kind donations; and shopping in the TCWF online mall.

WINGS

P.O. Box 95615
Palatine, IL 60095
Ph. 847-963-8910
www.wingsprogram.com

WINGS, which stands for Women In Need Growing Stronger, is an organization dedicated to serving women impacted by homelessness and domestic violence. This organization has 17 locations that serve women and children in the North and Northwest suburbs. Services offered include life skills development, financial counseling, vocational counseling, work re-entry, domestic violence safe-housing, legal advocacy, and more. Opportunities to volunteer include organizing and attending fundraising events like the Annual Come Fly with Me Gala; helping out in the resale store; and providing general office assistance.

YMCA

www.ymca.net

The YMCA helps people build healthy minds, bodies, and souls. The Y is the nation's largest non-profit community service organization that's dedicated to serving the health and social needs of local communities. Currently, this organization serves nearly 18 million people in over 10,000 communities and offers volunteer opportunities as unique as the communities it serves. Volunteers can lead exercise classes; read to pre-school children; coach a basketball team; organize special events; address neighborhood issues; and more. Specific needs vary by community. Log onto the Web site to find a 'Y' near you.

Y-ME National Breast Cancer Organization

203 N. Wabash, Suite 1220
Chicago, IL 60601
Ph. 1-800-221-2141
www.y-me.org/illinois

This organization is dedicated to minimizing the impact of breast cancer, creating awareness of the disease, and providing support to those faced with the illness. Volunteer opportunities include making phone calls or writing letters to law makers to influence votes on breast cancer related issues; and attending and promoting special events like the Y-Me Race, the Y-Me Annual Luncheon & Fashion Show, the Y-Me Young Professionals Ball, and the Pink Onederland—an event showcasing and selling unique creations around the holidays.

Volunteer
RESOURCES
in the City!

Chicago Volunteer.net

300 N. Elizabeth St.
Chicago, IL 60607
Ph. 312-491-7820
www.chicagovolunteer.net

Chicago Volunteer.net is one of the largest databases filled with thousands of volunteer opportunities. This database was developed and is maintained by Community Resource Network. Volunteer opportunities range from hands on projects such as adult literacy and park beautification, to serving on boards of non-profit organizations. If you're looking to give back to your community, this is a great place to find an opportunity that you'll enjoy. The database is easy to use, allowing you to search by cause, length of commitment, and location.

Compumentor

www.itresourcecenter.org

This organization offers volunteer opportunities to those with careers in IT. It matches volunteers with non-profit organizations in need of IT assistance.

Volunteer Match

www.volunteermatch.org

This database has a comprehensive listing of volunteer opportunities. Currently, it houses over 30,000 volunteer opportunities being offered by over 25,000 organizations. The organization helps individuals find great places to volunteer. Just type in your zip code and a listing of volunteer opportunities in your area will appear. You can also narrow your search by specifying your particular area of interest, skills and time available. This database offers literally thousands of volunteer opportunities in several categories including Advocacy and Human Rights, Hunger and Homelessness, Sports and Recreation, Board Development, Arts & Culture, Education and Literacy, Environment, and much more.

Reflexology

Pilates

Healthy

Travelers

Spa Bath

Chill Out!

Peaceful Places

Relax

Yoga

Massage

Stone Therapy

Thai Yoga

Reiki

Meditate

Chill Out! In the City

Chicago may be a busy, fast paced City, but there are tons of places to go if you ever want to just chill out or relax. In addition to offering tons of things to do to remain active, Chicago is home to some of the best day spas in the Midwest. When life becomes hectic and stressful, an urban oasis—whether it's a walk through a garden or a visit to a day spa—is all you need to boost your spirits and your energy levels. Visits to day spas and practicing yoga are my urban escapes. Once I've gotten a massage or a mud wrap, my batteries are re-charged and I feel as if I can take on the world. If I can't get to a spa, I'll take a yoga class and leave the yoga studio feeling completely balanced having cleared my mind and reflected upon what's important for me to get a life! Another thing I'll do to relax is take long walks. I remember once after a very stressful period at work, I took a day off and went to the Chicago Botanic Gardens. I had never been there so I was excited about going. Before my trip, I went to the store and purchased a disposable camera. When I arrived at the gardens, I took a tram tour of the entire area. After the tour, I walked around all day taking pictures of all the exotic flowers, plants, trees, sculptures, and waterfalls. Spending an entire day in nature and being surrounded by such beauty and vibrancy ignited my soul. I felt as if I was in a different world. I also noticed many older people in wheelchairs with their caretakers. I believe there's something to be said about the healing power of connecting with nature. When I went to work the next day, I felt like a new woman.

The following section lists day spas, yoga and pilates studios, and gardens in and around the City.

YOGA STUDIOS
in the City!

Temple of Kriya Chicago

2414 N. Kedzie Blvd.
Chicago, IL 60647
Ph. 773-342-4600
www.yogakriya.org

The Temple of Kriya has been around for over 30 years, teaching Hatha Yoga—a form of yoga that coordinates the body movement, breathing, and mental focus. There's also a yoga class called Restorative Yoga, which emphasizes deep relaxation. Day and evening classes are available. In addition to yoga classes, this organization also offers meditation and astrology classes.

Om on the Range

3759 N. Ravenswood #125
Chicago, IL 60613
Ph. 773-525-YOGA (9642)
www.omontherange.net

This yoga studio is dedicated to those interested in "hot yoga" or yoga in the Bikram tradition. Hot yoga is the practice of yoga in a studio heated to at 105F degrees. There are more gentle hot yoga classes where the studio is heated to only 95F degrees. Om on the Range was opened by a couple pondering what they wanted to do when they retired. They decided not to wait until they reached retirement age, and thus Om on the Range was born.

Chill Out! In the City

Bikram Yoga Chicago

1344 N. Milwaukee 3rd Floor
Chicago, IL 60622
Ph. 773-395-9150
www.bycic.com

There are several Bikram Yoga Studios located in Chicago and in the suburbs. These studios focus on Bikram Yoga or "hot yoga" where the yoga studio is heated to 105 F degrees. Beginners are welcomed to all classes, which are 90 minutes long. Classes are offered during the day and in the evening. To learn more about Bikram Yoga in general, visit www.Bikramyoga.com.

For the other Chicago location and the Naperville location, visit www.bikram citychicago.com and www.bikramyoganaperville.com

Yoga Circle

401 W. Ontario
Chicago, IL 60610
Ph. 312-915-0750
www.yogacircle.com

Located in Chicago's River North, Yoga Circle offers Iyengar Yoga instruction—a form of yoga that focuses on standing postures. There are classes for students who are new to the practice of yoga as well as classes for those who are more advanced. Classes are also offered during the day and in the evening.

Chicago Yoga Center

3047 N. Lincoln Ave. Suite 320
Chicago, IL 60657
Ph. 773-327-3650
www.yogamind.com

This yoga studio teaches various forms of yoga including Hatha, Iyengar, Ashtanga, and Yin Yoga. Located on the near Northside, this yoga studio offers yoga classes for all levels and has day, evening, and weekend hours. They also lead yoga workshops in exotic places such as Peru and India.

Global Yoga and Wellness Center

1823 W. North Ave.
Chicago, IL 60622
Ph. 773-489-1510
www.globalyogacenter.com

Located in the Wicker Park/Bucktown area, this yoga studio offers yoga classes in a variety of styles and traditions including Hatha Yoga, Vinyasa Yoga, Ashtanga Yoga, White Lotus Flow Yoga, and Anusara Yoga. Classes welcome both beginners and more experienced yoga students. There are also pre-natal yoga and mom and baby yoga classes offered.

Lincolnshire Yoga

39 Plymouth Ct.
Lincolnshire, IL 60069
Ph. 847-945-0808
www.lincolnshireyoga.bizland.com/

Lincolnshire Yoga teaches Hatha Yoga from basics to advanced. The philosophy at Lincolnshire Yoga is that each student should progress at his or her own pace. Emphasis is placed on relaxing, breathing, and meditating. There are three locations in the Lincolnshire area offering classes during the day and at night.

Yoga Now

5852 N. Broadway
Chicago, IL. 60660
Ph. 773-561-YOGA (9642)
www.yoganowchicago.com

This yoga studio offers a variety of classes including Mysore, Ashtanga, Vinyasa and Forrest Yoga. For beginners, there's Yoga Basics and for women who are expecting, there's Pre-natal Yoga. There's also an Open yoga class that is suitable for students of all levels and a dance class called 5Rythms Dancing for those who enjoy dancing. Classes are offered 7 days a week in the morning, afternoon and evening.

Yoga View

232 N. Clybourn Ave.
Chicago, IL. 60614
Ph. 773-883-YOGA (9642)
www.yogaview.com

Yoga View, a yoga studio dedicated to sharing the benefits of yoga to the City of Chicago, offers a wide variety of classes including Ashtanga, Mysore, Tibetan, Yantra, and Pre-natal Yoga. Classes are available for yoga students of all levels. Special workshops and retreats are also offered.

Sweet Pea's Studio (A family Yoga Center)

3717 N. Ravenswood #213
Chicago, IL. 60613
Ph. 773-248-YOGA (9642)
www.sweetpeasstudio.com

This studio specializes in yoga classes for expecting parents and parents with young children. Classes offered include Pre-natal, Post-partum, Family, and Hatha Yoga. Other classes include Pre and Post-natal Belly Dancing and infant massage. Taking yoga at this studio is a great way to introduce your family to the benefits and practice of yoga.

Moksha Yoga Center

700 N. Carpenter
Chicago, IL. 60622
Ph. 312-942-9642
www.mokshayoga.com

With locations in Riverwest, Lakeview, and the Gold Coast, Moksha Yoga Center offers a wide variety of classes including instruction in

Ashtanga, Mysore, and Vinyasa Yoga. In addition to classes, this yoga center offers special workshops, teacher trainings, retreats, and other special events.

PILATES STUDIOS
in the City!

A Body Within

3701 N. Ravenswood, Suite 204
Chicago, IL. 60613
Ph. 773-404-2412
www.abodywithin.com

This pilates studio teaches its students how to "empower" their bodies, minds and souls through movement. In addition to private pilates instruction, group classes are also offered in mat pilates. For those interested in teaching pilates, there is also teacher training available. Services that compliment the practice of pilates and support the mission of this studio include massage therapy.

Flow Inc.

2248 N. Clark St.
Chicago, IL. 60614
Ph. 773-975-7540
www.flowchicago.com

The owner of this yoga and pilates studio decided to call the studio "Flow" because she believes that by practicing pilates and yoga regularly, the mind and body will learn to flow in harmony which results in efficient use of energy. Classes offered here include Pilates Fundamentals, Pilates Matwork, Piloga (pilates and yoga combined), and Dance Condition. Private instruction is also available.

Frog Temple Pilates

1774 N. Damen Ave.
Chicago, IL. 60647
Ph. 773-489-0890
www.frogtemple.com

Frog Temple Pilates studio has been providing pilates instruction since 1999. Instructors here believe that practicing pilates can benefit people of all ages and abilities. They also believe that pilates can have a positive impact on the mind, body, and spirit. Classes offered include Mat Pilates, Piloga (pilates and yoga combined), Pilates on the Ball, Pilates for Runners, Pre-natal Pilates, and more. Teacher training and certification, special workshops, and private instruction are also available.

Body Endeavors

1528 N. Halsted
Chicago, IL. 60622
Ph. 312-202-0028
www.bodyendeavorspilates.com

Body Endeavors offers classes for beginners as well as advanced pilates students. There are also special packages available, including packages for brides to be who desire to be fit and lean for their big day. Other packages include a 10-week health and fitness challenge which includes personalized nutritional counseling, group and individual pilates sessions, free weights and cardio training, health and educational workshops, and much more. For those who want to teach pilates, certification classes are also available.

Power Pilates at Equinox

900 N. Michigan Ave.
Chicago, IL. 60611
Ph. 312-335-8464
www.powerpilates.com/studio/locations/900northmichigan.html

Power Pilates began in New York in 1989, branching out to Chicago and California. This organization now has two locations in Chicago—one located on the Mag Mile and the other located on Clark Street in the Equinox Fitness Centers. Each studio offers both private and semi-private pilates sessions that typically last for just under an hour. Both mat pilates and pilates using the pilates machine are offered.

From the Center Pilates Studio

3047 N. Lincoln Ave. Suite 310
Chicago, IL. 60657
Ph. 773-528-1099
www.fromthecenterpilates.com

This pilates studio offers both private and group sessions for clients who wish to recover from or prevent injury and keep fit. Each session lasts for 55 minutes. Other services include massage therapy, and shiatsu bodywork. For those who wish to teach pilates, this studio offers a teacher training program.

DAY
Spas
in the City!

The Peninsula Spa

108 E. Superior St.
Chicago, IL. 60611
Ph. 312-573-6860
www.peninsulaspachicago.com

Located in the luxurious Hotel Peninsula, this spa offers some of the finest spa services in the Windy City. The Peninsula Spa boasts an extensive selection of body treatments that rejuvenate the body and stimulate the senses such as the Cranberry Citrus Body Smoothie. In addition to body treatments, The Peninsula Spa offers a variety of massage therapies like Reflexology, Swedish massage, and Therapeutic massage. There are also spa treatments available for men.

Channing's Day Spa

54 E. Oak St.
Chicago, IL. 60611
Ph. 312-280-1994
www.channings.com

This cozy day spa, located in a Victorian townhouse on Oak Street has been helping Chicagoans relax for over 22 years by offering a wide range of services and special packages. Spa services include massage therapies like Swedish Stress Reliever, Aromatherapy Massage, and Heat Therapy Massage; spa manicures and pedicures for both men and women; and pregnancy massage. There are special packages designed for men, teenagers, and bridal parties.

Thousand Waves Spa for Women

1212 W. Belmont Ave.
Chicago, IL 60657
Ph. 773-549-0700
www.thoursandwavesspa.com

This is truly an urban escape for women that gives something back to the community. This day spa offers a stress management program for women who have cancer. The program provides free services including massage therapy and spa baths. Swedish Massage, Deep Tissue Massage, Hot Stone Massage, and Pre-natal Massage are among the massage therapies that all customers can choose from. Other treatments include herbal wraps and spa baths.

Urban Oasis

12 W. Maple St. 3rd Floor
Chicago, IL 60610
Ph. 312-587-3500
www.urbanoasis.biz

This day spa certainly lives up to its name. The atmosphere is very warm, inviting, and relaxing, making you forget about your worries as soon as you step through the door. Services focus on massage therapies which include Swedish massage, Deep Tissue Therapy, Reiki, Sports Massage, Pregnancy Massage, Aromatherapy Massage, Hot Stone Massage, and much more. In addition to the Maple Street location, there is also a location on North Avenue. Visit www.urbanoasis.biz for more details.

Soma Spa

3329 Vollmer Rd.
Flossmoor, IL 60422
Ph. 708-957-4400
www.thesomaspa.com

Soma Spa is truly a hidden gem in the South Suburbs that's worth finding and hanging onto. This day spa is one of my personal favorites, offering a wide range of therapies and treatments. Massage therapies include Swedish Massage, Therapeutic Massage, Sports Massage, Reflexology, Reiki, Thai Yoga Massage, and Pregnancy Massage. Body treatments include the Seaweed Envelope, Moor Mud, Aromatherapy Wrap, Body Polish, and more. Facials and Waxing are also available.

Asha Salon and Spa

1135 N. State St.
Chicago, IL 60610
Ph. 312-664-1600
www.ashasalonspa.com

Asha, which means life, is the perfect name for this salon and day spa which offers a wide range of services including massage therapy and body treatments. Massage therapies include Sports Massage, Hot Stone Massage, Baby Massage, Reflexology, and more. Body treatments include Aromatherapy Wrap and Body Polish. Other services include Spa Manicures, Spa Pedicures, facials, and make-up lessons. Bridal packages, Grooms packages, and other men's packages are also available. In addition to the State Street location, there is a location on Damen Ave. on the Northside as well as a location in Schaumburg.

Kaya Day Spa

112 N. May St., 2nd Floor
Chicago, IL 60607
Ph. 312-243-5292
www.kayadayspa.com

Kaya is the name for a Japanese tree, which is strong and resistant to stress. This 10,000 square foot day spa truly reflects its name. It is indeed beautiful and the treatments offered here can help anyone endure the stresses in their lives. The décor at Kaya Day Spa is modern and beautiful featuring a beverage bar, a cozy café, and even internet stations for those who just can't completely get away from their computers. Treatments include massage therapies, such as Deep Tissue Massage, Swedish Massage, Pre-natal Massage, Infant Massage, and more. Hydrotherapies offered include Meditation Bath, Rose Milk Bath, Vitamin C Bath, and Detoxification Bath, to name a few. Kaya also offers body treatments like the Moor Mud. There are special spa packages available for both men and women. Manicures, pedicures, and facials are also offered.

Spa Nordstrom

520 N. Michigan Ave.
Chicago, IL 60611
Ph. 312-379-4300
www.nordstrom.com

A day at Nordstrom, which includes a visit to Spa Nordstrom, has to be the ultimate treat. Let's face it, Shopping can be hard work, so why not reward yourself with a foot massage afterward? There are two Spa Nordstrom locations—one in the heart of downtown and the other in beautiful suburban Oakbrook. These full service day spas offer a full range of spa services. Body therapies include Satin Body Glow, Detox and Re-balancing, Tropical Smoothie, Algae Wrap, Mud Wrap, and Aromatherapy Wrap. Hydrotherapies include

Algae Marine Bath, Cleopatra Bath, Mustard Bath, Essential Oils Bath, and Oxygen Bath. Massage therapies include Reflexology, Shiatsu Massage, Spa Nordstrom Massage (Swedish Massage), Pre-natal Massage, Deep Tissue Massage, Sports Massage, Aromatherapy Massage, Spa Nordstrom Healing and Hot Stone Massage, Chair Massage, Craniosacral, Reiki, Lymphatic Massage, and Acupuncture. Facials, manicures, special spa packages, and treatments for men are also available.

Honey Child Salon and Spa

735 N. LaSalle Dr.
Chicago, IL 60610
Ph. 312-573-1955
www.honeychildsalonandspa.com

This is one of the sweetest day spas in Chicago. There are two locations offering a wide range of services and treatments. Massage therapies include Hot Honey on the Rocks, Deep Tissue Massage, Sports Massage, Swedish Massage Aromatherapy Massage, and Body Butter Massage. A wide range of body treatments is available like Beautiful Back Treatment, Honey Buns (an exfoliating body treatment for a soft backside), Mango Body Buff, Honey Drench Cocoon, and more. There are also hand and foot treatments like Reflexology, Honey Mango, Citrus Soak, Brown Sugar, Shea Butter and Cucumber Therapy to name a few. Men's treatments and bridal packages are available.

Chicago School of Massage Therapy
Professional and Student Clinic

1300 W. Belmont Ave.
Chicago, IL 60657
Ph. 773-880-1397
www.csmt.com

If you're looking for a place to get a great massage at affordable prices, this school is worth checking out. Clients can choose to have services performed by students supervised by instructors at a lower price or professional massage therapists at retail prices. Professional massage therapists offer Clinical Massage, Sports Massage, Pregnancy Massage, Relaxation Therapy, Myofacial Therapy, and Manual Lymph Drainage. Students perform Therapeutic Massage.

Spa Ariel

1111 S. Wabash Ave.
Chicago, IL 60605
Ph. 312-431-1573

Spa Ariel is one of Chicago's best-kept secrets. Located in the South Loop, this modern yet peaceful and inviting spa offers body treatments such as Gommage Marin (Body Polish), Phyto Marine (a detoxifying and Contouring treatment), and Silhouette Detox (a detoxifying herbal Wrap). Massage therapies include Deep Tissue Massage, Therapeutic Massage, Aroma Luxe, Relaxation Massage, Maternity Massage, and Stone Therapy Reflexology. Spa Ariel is also a great place to enjoy a manicure, pedicure or a facial.

Exhale Mind Body Spa

945 N. State St.
Chicago, IL 60610
Ph. 312-753-6500
www.exhalespa.com

This brand new modern, relaxing 9,400 square foot day spa is not only a great place to relax, it is also a great place to stretch and strengthen. In addition to traditional spa services, Exhale offers yoga and pilates classes, retreats, and workshops. Nutritional coaching is also offered. Spa services include massage therapies, body treatments, manicures, pedicures and facials. Exhale Fusion Massage, Deep Tissue Massage, Four Handed Massage, Thai Massage, Reflexology, and Reiki are among the massage therapies available. Rejuvenating body treatments include Body Detox Therapy, Body Enlightening, Craniosacral Therapy, and Acupuncture. Manicures and pedicures are also available. There's also a special 6-week program called Total Body Transformation, which combines various services such as pilates, yoga, Acupuncture, and nutritional coaching.

SPA
Alternatives
in the City!

Mobile Spa Chicago

www.mobilespachicago.com
Ph. 847-739-3106

Mobile Spa Chicago brings the spa to you. This is a great way to enjoy a girls' night in or a bachelorette party. Massage therapists, estheticians, nail technicians come out to your home, equipped with everything needed for a relaxing spa experience. Massage services include Swedish Massage, Sports Massage, Hot Stone Therapy, Motherhood Massage, Shiatsu Massage, and more. Body treatments such as the Seaweed Roll, Anti-cellulite Treatment, and Full-body Salt Glow are available.

Home Spa Sessions

www.homespasessions.com
Ph. 630-663-4001

Home Spa Sessions also comes right to your door to provide spa services. If you'd like, they will even provide catering. Services include massage therapies, facials, manicures and pedicures. Hot Stone Massage, Reiki, and Massage Delights, Milk and Honey Pedicure, and French Manicure are just a sampling of what Home Spa Sessions professionals can offer help you and your guests relax. If you don't feel like cooking, catering can be provided by Gourmet on the Move.

GARDENS & OTHER
Peaceful Places
in the City!

Osaka Garden in Jackson Park

6401 S. Stony Island
Chicago, IL 60617
Ph. 312-742-PLAY (7589)
www.chicagoparkdistrict.com

A beautiful Japanese Garden located in the Hyde Park/Jackson Park area. There's a beautiful bridge, stone paths, a waterfall and a peaceful stream. This garden is great for an early morning stroll.

Anderson Japanese Gardens

318 Spring Creek Rd.
Rockford, IL 61107
Ph. 815-229-9391
www.andersongardens.org

Open from May through October, this Japanese garden is very serene. There are beautiful bridges and waterfalls throughout the garden. This is a great place to take pictures. In fact, there are photography classes along with yoga and pilates classes offered. Group tours are available.

Lincoln Park Conservatory

2391 N. Stockton
Chicago, IL 60614
Ph. 312-742-7736
www.chicagoparkdistrict.com

Lincoln Park Conservatory is a great place to learn about exotic flowers such as orchids. The Palm House, The Fernery, the Orchid House and the Show House are the 4 major houses make up the conservatory. The Show House is where special exhibits and events are held.

The Morton Arboretum

4100 IL Rt. 53
Chicago, IL. 60532
Ph. 630-968-0074
www.mortonarb.org

The Morton Arboretum boasts 1,700 acres of beautiful gardens, plant collections, and natural areas (oak and maple forests). In addition to being a beautiful site, there are tons of things to do. There's a children's garden where kids can learn about nature and play. Twilight concerts are held where visitors can sit back and enjoy an evening picnic and some great music. There are also theatre hikes where visitors can enjoy great theatre in addition to some light exercise amid beautiful scenery.

Peggy Notebaert Nature Museum

2430 N. Canon Dr.
Chicago, IL. 60614
Ph. 773-755-5100
www.naturemuseum.org

The Peggy Notebaert Nature Museum is designed to inspire both kids and adults to learn more about and appreciate the environment. For anyone who loves butterflies, there is a 2,700 square foot greenhouse filled with various species. There are also a variety of animals such as turtles, snakes, salamanders, and newts that can be observed. This is a great place to bring the special kid in your life.

Chicago Botanic Gardens

1000 Lake Cook Rd.
Glencoe, IL. 60022
Ph. 847-835-5440
www.chicagobotanic.org

Located in the Northwest suburbs of Chicago, the Chicago Botanic Gardens is one of the most beautiful and peaceful places in the Chicago area. There are actually 26 gardens rolled into one. The types of gardens include a Japanese garden, fruit and vegetable garden, rose garden, circle garden featuring annuals, and much more. There are beautiful pathways and waterfalls throughout the grounds. If you're looking for a peaceful place filled with the vibrant colors of exotic flowers and the soothing sounds of gentle waterfalls, this is the place to go. Also, if you're looking to learn something about nature, cooking and even exercise, a variety of programs are offered including horticulture classes, cooking classes, gardening classes, and even yoga classes.

Garfield Park Conservatory

300 N. Central Park
Chicago, IL. 60624
Ph. 773-638-1776
www.garfieldconservatory.org

Located on Chicago's Westside, Garfield Park Conservatory is a one of the largest conservatories in the U.S. This conservatory is home to several species of plant life including cacti, ferns, palm trees, Azaleas, Chrysanthemums, and more. There are even fruit plants housed in the conservatory including mango, banana, pineapple, chocolate, and sugar cane.

Cuneo Museum & Gardens

1350 N. Milwaukee Ave.
Vernon Hills, IL. 60061
Ph. 847-362-3042
www.cuneomuseum.org

This museum and garden were once a residence. The museum, which is an Italian-style villa, sits on a breathtaking 80-acre estate. There are seasonal gardens on the grounds as well as a tropical plant conservatory. Cultural, educational, and theatrical programs are held here throughout the year. A children's art fair, the Classic Car Show, and Easter and Mother's Day Brunches are also held annually.

Bahai Temple

100 Linden Ave.
Wilmette, IL. 60091
Ph. 847-853-2300
www.us.bahai.org

This is perhaps one of the most gorgeous temples in the country featuring nine sides and a dome. It is a peaceful house of worship for people of all races, creeds, and religions. The outside is just as beautiful as the inside, with gardens and fountains dispersed throughout the grounds.

By Topic!

Running

Biking

Ski

Sailing

Kayak

Canoeing

Martial Arts

Yoga

Training

Marathon

Kickboxing

Arts Crafts & More

Leagues

Arts, Crafts, and More
in the City!

Archeworks

625 N. Kingsbury St.
Chicago, IL 60610
Ph. 312-867-7254
Fax 312-867-7260
www.archeworks.org

artScape Chicago

66 E. Randolph St.
Chicago, IL 60601
Ph. 312-744-8925 Fax 312-744-9249
www.Gallery37.org/adult/artscape

Bauhaus Apprenticeship Institute

1757 N. Kimball Ave.
Chicago, IL 60651
Ph.773-235-7951
http://lf.org/bhai2000/

Cole Studio

410 S. Michigan Ave., Suite 306
Chicago, IL 60605
Ph. 312-362-9890
www.gracecole.com

The Drawing Workshop

4410 N. Ravenswood Ave.
Chicago, IL 60613
Ph. 773-728-1127

DuPage Art League

218 W. Front St.
Wheaton, IL 60187
Ph. 630-653-7090
www.dupageartleague.org

Ed Hinkley Watercolor Classes & Workshops

4052 N. Western Ave.
Chicago, IL 60618
Ph. 773-539-6047

Evanston Art Center

2603 Sheridan Rd.
Evanston, IL 60201
Ph. 847-475-5300
Fax 847-475-5330
www.evanstonartcenter.org

Fire Arts Center of Chicago

1800 W. Cuyler Street
Chicago, IL 60613
Ph. 773-271-7710
www.firearts.org

Gallery 37

66 E. Randolph St.
Chicago, IL 60601
Ph. 312-744-8925/Fax 312-744-9249
www.Gallery37.or

Glass Frog Studio

775 W. Jackson Blvd., 5th Floor
Chicago, IL 60661
Ph. 773-454-3456
Fax 312-733-0072
www.glassfrogstudio.com

Hyde Park Art Center

5307 S. Hyde Park Blvd.
Chicago, IL 60615
Ph. 773-324-5520
Fax 773-324-6641
www.hydeparkart.org

J. Miller Handcrafted Furniture

1774 W. Lunt Ave.
Chicago, IL 60626
Ph. 773-761-3311
Fax 773-761-7546
www.furnituremaking.com

La Grange Art League

122 Calendar Ct.
La Grange, IL 60525
Ph. 708-352-1480
www.lagrangeartleague.org

Lill Street Art Center

4401 N. Ravenswood
Chicago, IL 60640
Ph. 773-769-4226
www.lillstreet.com

Northshore Art League

620 Lincoln Ave.
Winnetka, IL 60093
Ph. 847-446-2870
www.northshoreartleague.org

Oak Park Art League

720 Chicago Ave.
Oak Park, IL 60302
Ph. 708-386-9853
Fax 708-386-4893
www.opal-art.com

Old Town Art Center

1763 N. North Park Ave.
Chicago, IL 60614
Ph. 312-337-1938
Fax 312-337-4015
www.oldtowntriangle.com

Ox-Bow

37 S. Wabash
Chicago, IL 60603
Ph. 1-800-318-3019
www.ox-bow.org

Palette & Chisel Academy of Fine Arts

1012 N. Dearborn Pkwy.
Chicago, IL 60610
Ph. 312-642-4400
Fax 312-642-4317
www.paletteandchisel.org

Riverside Arts Center

32 E. Quincy St.
Riverside, IL 60546
Ph. 708-442-6400
www.riversideartscenter.com

Suburban Fine Arts Center

1957 Sheridan Rd
Highland Park, IL 60035
Ph. 847-432-1888
Fax 847-432-9106
www.sfac.net

Terra Incognito Studios & Gallery

246 Chicago Ave.
Oak Park, IL 60302
Ph. 708-383-6228
www.terraincongitostudios.com

The School of the Art Institute of Chicago

37S. Wabash Ave.
Chicago, IL 60603
Ph. 312-899-5100
www.artic.edu

TLD Design Center & Gallery

26 E. Quincy St.
Westmont, IL 60559
Ph. 630-963-9573
www.tlddesigns.com

Triangle Camera, Inc.

3445 N. Broadway
Chicago, IL 60657
Ph. 773-472-1015
www.trianglecamera.com

Vital Projects, Ltd.

1579 N. Milwaukee Ave.,
Suite 230
Chicago, IL 60622
Ph. 773-489-0455
Fax 773-489-0481
www.vitalprojects.com

Act One Studios

640 N. LaSalle St.,
Suite. 535Chicago, IL 60610
Ph. 312-787-9384
www.actone.com

The Actor's Gymnasium

927 Noyes St.
Evanston, IL 60201
Ph. 847-328-2795
Fax 847-328-3495
www.actorsgymnasium.com

The Audition Studio

20 W. Hubbard, Suite 2E
Chicago, IL 60610
Ph. 312-527-4566
www.theauditionstudio.com

Barbizon

1051 Perimeter Dr., Suite 950
Schaumburg, IL 60173
Ph. 847-240-4200/Fax 847-413-2099
www.modelsmidwest.com

Chicago Access Network (CAN TV)

22 S. Green St., Suite 100
Chicago, IL 60607
Ph. 312-738-1400
Fax 312-738-2519
www.cantv.org

Chicago Center for Performing Arts

777 N. Green St.
Chicago, IL 60622
Ph. 312-327-2040
www.theaterland.com

Chicago Dramatists

1105 W. Chicago Ave.
Chicago, IL 60622
Ph. 312-633-0630
www.chicagodramatists.org

Chicago Filmmakers

5243 N. Clark St., 2nd Floor
Chicago, IL 60640
Ph. 773-293-1447/Fax 773-293-0575
www.chicagofilmmakers.org

Comedy College

2951 N. Greenview
Chicago, IL 60657
Ph. 773-250-7979
www.comedycollegeinfo.com

Comedy Sportz

2851 N. Halsted St.
Chicago, IL 60657
Ph. 773-549-8080 ext. 224
Fax 773-549-8142
www.comedysportzchicago.com

Community Film Workshop

1130 South Wabash, Suite 302
Chicago, IL 60605
Ph. 312-427-1245/Fax 312-427-8818
www.cfwchicago.org

Piven Theatre Workshop

927 Noyes St.
Evanston, IL 60201
Ph. 847-866-6597
www.piventheatre.org

The Screenwriters Group

1803 W. Byron
Chicago, IL 60613
Ph. 773-665-8500
Fax 773-665-9475
www.screenwritersgroup.com

Voice Power/Helen Cutting

445 E. Ohio St., Suite 1914
Chicago, IL 60611
Ph. 312-527-1809
www.voicepowr.com

Cooking *in the City!*

The American Institute of Wine & Food Chicago Chapter

Ph. 312-440-9290

Calphalon Culinary Center

1000 W. Washington St.
Chicago, IL 60607
Ph. 312-529-0100/Fax 866-623-2089
www.calphalonculinarycenter.com

Coachouse Gourmet

Ph. 847-724-1521
www.coachousegourmet.com

Cook From Scratch

PO Box 543877
Chicago, IL 60654
Ph. 312-559-0052/Fax 312-655-0767
www.cookfromscratch.com

Cooking with Best Chefs

1N446 Goodrich Ave.
Glen Ellyn, IL 60137
Ph. 630-793-0600/Fax 630-793-0288
www.BestChefs.com

Chefs On Call

Chicago, IL 60614
Ph. 312-787-9451
www.chefsoncall.com

Chez Madelaine School of Cooking & Cooking Tours

Ph. 630-655-0355
www.chezm.com

ChicaGourmets

www.chicagourmets.com
Ph. 708-383-7543/Fax 708-383-4964

Chopping Block Cooking School

1324 W. Webster Ave.
Chicago, IL 60614
Ph. 773-472-6700
www.thechoppingblock.net

College of DuPage County

425 Fawall Blvd.
Glen Ellyn, IL 60137
Ph. 630-942-2208 or 630-942-2800
www.cod.edu/conted

Culinary Historian of Chicago

2113 Sanborn Circle
Plainfield, IL 60544
Ph. 815-439-3960
www.culinaryhistorians.org

Elgin Community College

1700 Spartan Dr.
Elgin, IL 60123
Ph. 847-622-3036
www.elgin.edu

French Culinary Experience

281 Messner Dr.
Wheeling, IL 60090
Ph. 847-215-1931
www.frenchcookingschool.com

International Kitchen

330 N. Wabash, Suite 3005
Chicago, IL 60611
Ph. 312-726-4525 or 800-945-8606
www.theinternationalkitchen.com

Italidea

500 N. Michigan Ave., Suite 1450
Chicago, IL 60611
Ph. 312-832-9545
Fax 312-822-9622
www.iicch.org

Kendall College

2408 Orrington Ave.
Evanston, IL 60201
Ph. 847-448-2550
www.kendall.edu

Rustic Kitchen

723 West Brompton Ave., Suite 2W
Chicago, IL 60657
Ph. 773-935-4239
www.rustickitchen.com

Sur La Table Culinary Center

52-54 E. Walton St.
Chicago, IL 60611
Ph. 312-337-0600/Fax 312-337-7454
www.surlatable.com

Whole Foods

www.wholefoods.com

Williams & Sonoma

900 N. Michigan Ave.
Chicago, IL 60611
Ph. 312-587-8080

World Kitchen

66 E. Randolph St.
Chicago, IL 60601
Ph. 312-742-8497 or 312-744-8925
Fax 312-744-9249
www.worldkitchenchicago.org

Cooking **Resources** *in the City!*

ChicagoCooks.com

www.chicagocooks.com

Slow Food

www.slowfoodusa.org

Languages & CULTURES *in the City!*

Alliance Française de Chicago

810 N. Dearborn St.
Chicago, IL 60610
Ph. 312-337-1070
Fax 312-337-3019
www.afchicago.com

Authentic Middle East Belly Dance

PO Box 56037
Chicago, IL 60656
Ph. 773-693-6300
Fax 773-693-6302
www.jasminjahal.com

Belle Plaine Studio

2014 W. Belle Plaine
Chicago, IL 60618
Ph. 773-935-1890/Fax 773-935-1909

Chicago Dance

3660 W. Irving Park Rd.
Chicago, IL 60618
Ph. 773-267-3421/Fax 773-267-1084
www.chicagodance.com

Joel Hall Dance Center

1511 West Berwyn
Chicago, IL 60640
773-293-0900
www.joelhall.org

French Institute of the North Shore

562 Green Bay Rd.
Winnetka, IL 60093
Ph. 847-501-5800/Fax 847-501-5855
www.FrenchInstituteNS.com

French Accents

3755 N. Western Ave.
Chicago, IL 60618
773-490-2141
www.frenchaccents.org

Instituto Cervantes Chicago

875 N. Michigan Ave., Suite 2940
Chicago, IL 60611
Ph. 312-335-1996
Fax 312-587-1992
www.cervantes1.org

Intrax English Institute

174 N. Michigan Ave., 2nd Fl
Chicago, IL 60601
Ph. 312-236-3208
Fax 312-236-3246
www.intraxenglish.com

Italidea

500 N. Michigan Ave.
Chicago, IL 60611
Ph. 312-832-4053
Fax 312-822-9622
www.italidea.org

Japanese Culture Center

1016 W. Belmont Ave.
Chicago, IL 60657
Ph. 773-525-3141
Fax 773-525-5916
www.japaneseculturecenter.com

Latin Street Dancing

540 N. LaSalle St., Suite 500
Chicago, IL 60610
Ph. 312-42-SALSA/312-427-2572
Fax 312-527-9238
www.laboriqua.com

McDonald Dance Academy

34 S. Evergreen
Arlington Heights, IL 60005
Ph. 847-342-1060
www.mcdonalddance.com

Natya Dance Theatre

410 South Michigan Ave., Suite 725
Chicago, IL 60605
Phone: (312) 212-1240
FAX (312) 212-1250
www.natya.com

Spanish Circle

10 W. Hubbard St., Suite 3E
Chicago, IL 60610
312-832-1282 or 773-525-9808
www.spanishcircle.com

Spanish Horizons

2526 N. Lincoln Ave. Ste 219
Chicago, IL 60614
Ph. 773-769-6300/773-348-7686
Fax 773-348-8518
www.spanishhorizons.com

Spanish Studios

722 W. Diversey Ave.
Chicago, IL 60614
Ph. 773-348-2216/Fax 773-435-2119
www.spanishstudio.com

The School of Ballet Chicago

218 S. Wabash St., 3rd Fl
Chicago, IL 60604
Ph. 312-251-8838/Fax 312-251-8840
www.balletchicago.org

The Henry George School of Social Science

417 S. Dearborn, Suite 510
Chicago, IL 60605
Ph. 312-362-9302
www.hgchicago.org

Philosophy,
Social Science &
WRITING
in the City!

Newberry Library

60 W. Walton St.
Chicago, IL 60610
Ph. 312-255-3700/Fax 312-255-3680
www.newberry.org

The Feltre School

22 W. Erie St.
Chicago, IL 60610
Ph. 312-255-1133
Fax 312-255-1378
www.feltre.org

Guild Complex

1532 N. Milwaukee Ave.
Chicago, IL 60622
Ph. 773-227-6117/Fax 773-227-6159
www.guildcomplex.com

StoryStudio Chicago

3717 N. Ravenswood, Suite 115
Chicago, IL 60613
Ph. 773-728-8441
www.storystudiochicago.com

Writers Digest School/Writers OnlineWorkshop.com

4700 E. Galbraith Rd.
Cincinnati, OH 45236
Ph. 1-800-759-0963
www.writersdigest.com/wds

WritingClasses.com (Gotham Writer's Workshop)

1841 Broadway, Suite 809
New York, NY 10023
Ph. 877-WRITERS
Fax 212-307-6325
www.writingclasses.com

MUSIC
in the City!

Allegro Music Studio

5301 N. Clark St.
Chicago, IL 60640
Ph. 773-334-4650
www.allegromusicstudio.com

Bloom School of Jazz

218 S. Wabash Ave., Suite 600
Chicago, IL 60604
Ph. 312-957-9300
Fax 312-957-013
www.bloomschoolofjazz.com

Old Town School of Folk Music

4544 N. Lincoln Ave.
Chicago, IL60625
Ph. 773-728-6000
www.oldtownschool.org

The Peoples Music School

931 W. Eastwood
Chicago, IL 60640
Ph. 773-784-7032
Fax 773-784-7134
www.peoplesmusicschool.org

Adult Continuing EDUCATION
in the City!

College of DuPage

425 Fawell Blvd.
Glen Ellyn, IL 60137
Ph. 630-942-2208
www.cod.edu

Harper College

1200 W. Algonquin Rd.
Palatine, IL 60067
Ph. 847-925-6300
www.harpercollege.edu

The Discovery Center

2940 N. Lincoln Ave.
Chicago, IL 60657
Ph. 773-348-8120
www.discoverycenter.cc

The Graham School

1427 East 60th St.
Chicago, IL 60637
Ph. 773-702-1722
www.grahamschool.uchicago.edu

The Norris Center at Northwestern University

1999 S. Campus Dr.
Evanston, IL 60208
Ph. 847-491-2301
www.norris.northwestern.edu/
minicourses.php

Oakton Community College

1600 E. Golf Rd.
Des Plaines, IL60016
Ph. 847-635-1600
www.oakton.edu

Prairie State College

202 S. Halstead St.
Chicago Heights, IL 60411
Ph. 708-709-3500
www.prairie.cc.il.us

Moraine Valley Community College

10900 S. 88th Ave.
Palos Hills, IL 60465
Ph. 708-974-4300
www.morainevalley.edu

Personal Growth/ SELF-HELP *in the City!*

Innerconnections

708 Church St., Suite 258
Evanston, IL 60201
Ph. 847-864-3730/Fax 847-256-8150
www.innerconnections.cc

Institute for Spiritual Leadership

5498 S. Kimbark
PO Box 53147
Chicago, IL 60653
Ph. 877-844-9440/Fax 773-752-5964
www.spiritleader.org

Wright Institute for Lifelong Learning

455 E. Ohio St., Suite 260
Chicago, IL 60611
Ph. 312-329-1200/Fax 312-645-8333
www.exceptionalliving.com

Running

in the City!

Arlington Trotters Running Club

Ph. 847-670-8331 or 847-368-0887
www.geocities.com/arltrotter

Alpine Runners

Ph. 847-438-8843
www.alpinerunners.com

Chicago Hash House Harriers

3155 N. Hudson
Chicago, IL, 60657
Ph. 312-409-BEER (2337)
www.chicagohash.com

Chicago Walkers Club

www.chicagowalkers.com

Evanston Running Club

PO Box 5329
Evanston, IL 60201
Ph. 847-869-8234
www.evanstonrunningclub.org

Fox River Trail Runners

PO Box 371
Geneva, IL 60134
Ph. 630-208-6677
www.frtr.org

Fleet Feet Running Groups

210 W. North Ave.
Chicago, IL 60610
Ph. 312-587-3338
www.fleetfeetchicago.com

Frontrunners/Frontwalkers Chicago

PO Box 148313
Chicago, IL 60614
Ph. 312-409-2790
www.frfwchicago.org

Lake Forest-Lake Bluff Running Club

www.lflb.org

Life Time Fitness Running Clubs

www.lifetimefitness.com

Lincoln Park Pacers

PO Box 14835
Chicago, IL 60614
Ph. 773-472-2344
www.lincolnparkpacers.org

Lisle Windrunners

PO Box 1171
Lisle, IL 60532
Ph. 630-585-4695
www.windrunners.org

Hillstriders Running Club

PO Box 1695
Crystal Lake, IL 60039
Ph. 815-455-4290
www.hillstriders.com

Niles West/Oakton Runners Club

www.nileswestoaktonrunnersclub.com

Oak Park Runners Club

PO Box 2322
Oak Park, IL
Ph. 708-848-3365
www.oprc.net

Park Forest Running & Pancake Club

PO Box 442
Park Forest, IL 60466
Ph. 708-802-2759
www.lincolnnet.net/pfrp

Polish Marathon Club of Chicago

Ph. 708-583-0494 or 630-370-7677
www.marathonpl.com

RunBig Chicago

www.orik.com/runbig
PO Box 1826
Oak Park, IL 60304-1826

Running
Resources
in the City!

AATRA—All American Trail Running Association

PO Box 9454
Colorado Springs, CO 80932
www.trailrunner.com
719-573-4405

American Running Association

4405 E. West Hwy, Suite 405
Bethesda, MD 20814
Ph. 1-800-776-2732
www.americanrunning.org

CARA

203 N.Wabash Ave., Suite 1104
Chicago, IL 60601
Ph. 312-666-9836
www.cararuns.org

RRCA—Road Runners Club America

8965 Guilford Rd., Suite 150
Columbia, MD 21046
Ph. 410-290-3890
www.rrca.org

USA Track & Field

1 RCA Dome Suite 140
Indianapolis, IN 46225
Ph. 317-261-0500
www.usatf.org

Running USA

5522 Camino Cerrallo
Santa Barbara, CA 93111
Ph. 805-964-0608
www.runningusa.org

Biking
in the City!

Bicycle Club of Lake County

PO Box 521
Libertyville, IL 60048
Ph. 847-604-0520
www.bikebclc.com

Chicago Cycling Club

PO Box 1178
Chicago, IL 60690
Ph. 773-509-8093
www.chicagocyclingclub.org

Elmhurst Bicycle Club

P.O. Box 902
Elmhurst, IL 60126
Ph. 630-415-BIKE (2453)
www.elmhurstbicycling.org

Folks on Spokes

P.O. Box 763
Matteson, IL 60443
Ph. 708-585-7672
www.folksonspokes.com

Schaumburg Bicycle Club

PO Box 68353
Schaumburg, IL 60168
Ph. 630-668-5204
www.schaumburgbicycleclub.org

Wheeling Wheelmen

P.O. Box 7304
Buffalo Grove, IL 60089
Ph. 847-520-5010
www.wheelmen.com

Multi-
SPORTS
in the City!

Chicago Area Orienteering Club

PO Box 0425
Chicago, IL 60690
Ph. 847-604-4419
www.chicago-orienteering.org

Water
SPORTS
in the City!

Columbia Yacht Club

111 N. Lake Shore Dr.
Chicago, IL 60601
Ph. 312-938-3625 | www.columbiay
achtclub.com

Jackson Park Yacht Club

6400 Promontory Dr.
Chicago, IL 60649
Ph. 773-684-5522
www.jpyc.org

Kayak Chicago

917 Southport Ave.
Lisle, IL 60532
Ph. 630-336-7245
www.kayakchicago.com

Lincoln Park Boat Club

P.O. Box 380
2506 N. Clark Street
Chicago, IL 60614
Ph. 773-549-2628
www.lpbc.net

Chicago River Rowing Club

Ph. 312-616-0056
www.chicagorowing.org

Chicago Sailing Club

2712 N. Campbell
Chicago, IL 60647
Ph. 773-871-SAIL
www.chicagosailingclub.com

Chicago Yacht Club

400 E. Monroe St.
Chicago, IL 60603
Ph. 312-861-7777
www.chicagoyachtclub.com

Northwest Passage

1130 Greenleaf Ave.
Wilmette, IL 60091
Ph.1-800-RECREATE (732-7328)
www.nwpassage.com

Prairie State Canoeists

www.prairiestatecanoeists.org

Chicago Friars Ski and Bike Club

www.chicagofriars.com

Fleetwind Ski Club

PO Box 607811
Chicago, IL 60660-7811
Ph. 630-415-3257
www.skifleetwind.com

Grand Prix Ski Club

5459 W. Wilson Ave.
Chicago, IL 60630
Ph. 773-777-8429
www.grandprixskiclub.com

Hustlers Ski Club

P.O. Box 91896
Elk Grove Village, IL 60009
Ph. 847-289-4644
www.hustlersskiclub.com

Ibex Ski & Snowboard Club

PO Box 1542
Palatine, IL 60078
Ph. 847-358-3385
www.members.aol.com/ibexskier

Lake Shore Ski Club

www.lssc.org

Lincoln Park Ski Club

PO Box 146405
Chicago, IL 60614
Ph.312-337-CLUB
www.lincolnparkskiclub.org

Nordic Fox Ski Club

PO Box 5615
Naperville, IL 60567
www.nordicfox.org

Oak Park Ski Club

P.O. Box 1162
Des Plaines, IL 60017
www.oakparkskiclub.org

Over the Hill Gang

1324 Fredrickson Place
Highland Park, IL 60035
Ph. 847-831-2965
www.chicagolandothgskiclub.com

Piccadilly Ski Club

PO Box 161
Clarendon Hills, IL 60514
Ph. 630-420-0040
www.piccadillyskiclub.com

Pine Point Ski Club

http://members.tripod.com/ddreier

Skunk Hollow Ski and Snowboard Club

www.skunkhollowskiclub.com

Chicago Metropolitan Ski Council

www.skicmsc.com

Leagues
in the City!

Chicago Sports Monster

4237 N. Western Ave.
Chicago, IL 60618
Ph. 773-866-2955
www.sportsmonster.net

Chicago Sport & Social Club

1516 N. Fremont
Chicago, IL 60622
Ph. 312-335-9596
www.chicagosportandsocialclub.com

Chicago Park District

Ph. 312-742-PLAY
www.chicagoparkdistrict.com

Players Sports

3347 N. Southport
Chicago, IL 60657
Ph. 773-528-1999
www.playerssports.net

Training
GROUPS
in the City!

Bulldog Bootcamp

4305 N. Lincoln
Chicago, IL 60618
Ph. 1-866-WoofWoof
www.bulldogbootcamp.com

Jeff Galloway Marathon Training

2800 N. Diversey
Chicago, IL
Ph. 773-509-4922
www.jeffgalloway.com

MaxFitness

312-327-6666
www.maxfitchicago.com

Union Station Multiplex Marathon Training

444 W. Jackson Blvd.
Chicago, IL 60606
Ph. 312-627-0444
www.multiplexclubs.com

Maratahon Training
for a
Good Cause
in the City!

Joints in Motion

29 E. Madison, Suite 500
Chicago, IL 60602
Ph. 312-372-2080 ext. 12
www.arthritis.org

Team Diabetes

30 N. Michigan Ave., Suite 2015
Chicago, IL 60602
Ph. 312-346-1805
www.diabetes.org

Team in Training

651 W. Washington Blvd, Suite 400
Chicago, IL 60661
Ph. 312-651-7350 ext. 240
www.teamintraining.org

Train to End Stroke

www.strokeassociation.org

Triathalon Training,
GROUPS
in the City!

Chicago Tri Club

P.O. Box 06198
Chicago, IL 60606
Ph. 312-944-4113
www.chicagotriclub.com

Tri-Masters Sports Initiative Programs

1448 E. 52nd St.
P.O. Box 172
Chicago, IL 60615
Ph. 773-995-2082
www.trimasters.org

Special Interest & Professional Organizations *in the City!*

20th Century Railroad Club

PO Box 476
Wilmette, IL 60091
Ph. 312-829-4500
www.20thcentury.org

American Association of Individual Investors (AAII)

Ph. 1-800-428-2244
www.aaii.com

American Business Women's Association

Ph.1-866-281-2143
www.abwa-chicago.org

Association of Information Technology Professionals

P.O. Box 809189
Chicago, IL 60680-9189
Ph. 312-245-1070
www.aitpchicago.com

American Association of University Women

1111 Sixteenth St. N.W.
Washington, DC 20036
Ph. 800-326-AAUW
www.aauw.org

American Marketing Association

311 S. Wacker Drive, Suite 5800
Chicago, IL 60606
Ph. 312-542-9000
www.marketingpower.com

Amnesty International

Midwest Regional Office
53 E. Jackson, Ste 731
Chicago, IL 60604
Ph. 312-427-2060
www.amnestyusa.org

Business Marketing Association

1920 N. Clark St. Suite 10A
Chicago, IL 60614
Ph. 312-943-8040
www.bmachicago.org

Socializing, Networking & DATING *in the City!*

Chicago Association of Direct Marketers

203 N.Wabash Ave., Suite 2100
Chicago, IL 60601
312-849-CADM
www.cadm.org

Chicago Council on Foreign Relations

332 S. Michigan Ave.
Chicago, IL 60604
Ph. 312-726-3860
www.ccfr.org

Independent Writers of Chicago

PMB 119
5465 W. Grand Ave., Suite 100
Gurnee, IL 60031
Ph. 847-855-6670
www.iwoc.org

International Trade Club of Chicago

Ph. 312-368-9197
www.itcc.org

Kiwanis International

3636 Woodview Trace
Indianapolis, IN 46268
Ph. 317-875-8755
www.kiwanis.org

Latin American Chamber of Commerce

3512 West Fullerton
Chicago, IL 60647
Ph. 773-252-5211
www.LACC1.com

National Association for Investors Corporation (NAIC)

Ph.1-877-275-6242
www.better-investing.org

National Black MBA Association

P.O. Box 8513
Chicago, IL 60680
Ph. 312-458-9161
www.ccnbmbaa.org

The Chicago Urban League

4510 S. Michigan Ave.
Chicago, IL 60653
773-285-5800
www.cul-chicago.org

Chicago Women in Publishing

P.O. Box 268107
Chicago, IL 60626
Ph. 312-641-6311
www.cwip.org

Chicago Advertising Federation

4700 West Lake Ave.
Glenview, IL 60025
Ph. 847-375-4728
www.chicagoadfed.org

Chicago Gay & Lesbian Chamber of Commerce

1210 W. Rosedale
Chicago, IL 60660
Ph. 773-303-0167
www.GLChamber.org

Chicago Songwriters Collective

www.chicagosongwriters.com

Chicago Association of Women Business Owners

330 South Wells Street, Suite 1110
Chicago, IL 60606
Ph. 312-322-0990
www.nawbochicago.org

Chicagoland Chamber of Commerce

One IBM Plaza
330 N. Wabash, Suite 2800
Chicago, IL 60611
Ph. 312-494-6700
www.chicagolandchamber.org

Chicago Professional Networking Association

P.O.Box 146368
Chicago, IL 60614
Ph. 773-296-CPNA (2762)
www.cpna.org

The Chicago Urban League

4510 S. Michigan Ave.
Chicago, IL 60653
773-285-5800
www.cul-chicago.org

International Trade Club of Chicago

Ph. 312-368-9197
www.itcc.org

Jaycees

P.O. Box 7
Tulsa, OK 74102
Ph. 1-800-JAYCEES
www.usjaycees.org

Highlife Adventures, Inc.

3047 N. Lincoln Ave. Suite 202
Chicago, IL 60657
Ph. 773-327-FUNN
www.highlifeadventures.com

Chicago Social Monster Sports Monster

4237 N. Western Ave.
Chicago, IL 60618
Ph. 773-866-2955 or 773-313-0038
www.socialmonster.com

Midwest Adventure's Traveler's Society

P.O. Box 1189
Chicago, IL 60690-1189
www.midwestats.org

First Friday's @ The Museum of Contemporary Art

220 E. Chicago Ave.
Chicago, IL 60611
Ph. 312-280-2260
www.mcachicago.org

Evening Associates with the Art Institute of Chicago

111 South Michigan Ave.
Chicago, IL 60603
Ph. 312-443-3600
www.artic.edu

Chicago Shakers Social & Adventure Club

Ph. 773-404-7067
www.chicagoshakers.com

Lincoln Park Young Professionals

1918 N. Cleveland Suite D
Chicago, IL 60614
Ph. 312-642-5097
www.lp-yp.com

Willow Creek Church Young Adult Ministry and Single Adult Ministry

67 E. Algonquin Rd.
South Barrington, IL 60010
Ph. 847-765-5000 ext. 1026
www.willowcreek.org

The Discovery Center

2940 N. Lincoln Ave.
Chicago, IL 60657
Ph. 773-348-8120
www.discoverycenter.cc

Singles Dining
CLUBS
in the City!

Single Gourmet Dining & Travel Club

29020 W. Grand Ave., Suite 100
Chicago, IL 60622
Ph. 773-772-3535
www.singlegourmetchicago.com

8 at 8 Dinner Club

P.O. Box 147251
Chicago, IL 60614
Ph. 312-583-0888
www.8at8.com

Gourmet Advocates/Club Suburbia

1414 W. Byron St., Suite 2E
Chicago, IL 60613
Ph.773-929-6534
www.gourmetadvocates.com

Charities/Volunteer
Opportunities
in the City!

20/30 Club

858 W. Armitage, Suite 175
Chicago, IL 60614
Ph. 312-409-3454
www.2030club.org

American Cancer Society

77 E. Monroe, 12th Floor
Chicago, IL 60603
Ph. 312-372-0471
www.cancer.org

American Diabetes Association

30 N. Michigan Ave., Suite 2015
Chicago, IL 60602
Ph. 312-346-1805
www.diabetes.org

Art Institute of Chicago

111 S. Michigan Ave.
Chicago, IL 60603
Ph. 312-443-3600
www.artic.edu

Aunt Martha's Youth Centers

233 W. Joe Orr Rd., North Bldg
Chicago Heights, IL 60411
Ph. 708-754-1044
www.auntmarthas.org

Big Brother/Big Sister

28 E. Jackson St., Suite 1800
Chicago, IL 6060
Ph. 312-427-0637
www.bbbschgo.org

Bottomless Closet

445 N. Wells, Suite 301
Chicago, IL 60601
Ph. 312-527-9664
www.bottomlesscloset.org

Brookfield Zoo

3300 Golf Rd.
Brookfield, IL 60513
Ph. 708-485-0263
www.brookfieldzoo.org

Cabrini Green Tutoring Program, Inc.

1515 N. Halsted St.
Chicago, IL 60622
Ph. 312-397-9119
www.cabrinigreentutoring.org

Chicago Abused Women's Coalition

P.O. Box 477916
Chicago, IL 60647
Ph. 773-489-9081
www.cawc.org

Chicago Architecture Foundation

224 S. Michigan Ave.
Chicago, IL 60604
Ph. 312-922-3432
www.architecture.org

Chicago Cares

300 W. Adams, Suite 300
Chicago, IL 60606
Ph. 312-780-0800
www.chicagocares.org

Chicago Food Depository

4100 W. Ann Lurie Place
Chicago, IL 60632
Ph. 773-247-3663
www.chicagosfoodbank.org

Chicago Greeters
Chicago Office of Tourism
78 East Washington Street
Chicago, IL 60602
Ph. 312-742-1190
www.chicagogreeter.com

Chicago Park Districts
Ph. 312-742-PLAY
www.chicagoparks.com

Chicago Youth Centers
104 S. Michigan Ave.
Chicago, IL 60603
Ph. 312-795-3500
www.chicagoyouthcenters.org

Cystic Fibrosis Foundation
www.cff.org

Earthwatch
Ph. 630-369-5186
http://earthwatch.chicago.home.att.net/

Friends of the Parks
55 E. Washington St., Suite 1911
Chicago, IL 60602
Ph. 312-857-2757
www.fotp.org

Fairy Godmother Foundation
1341 W. Fullerton Ave., Box 179
Chicago, IL 60614
Ph. 773-388-1160
www.fairygodmother.org

Field Museum
1400 S. Lake Shore Dr.
Chicago, IL 60605
Ph. 312-922-9410
www.fmnh.org

Gallery 37
66 E. Randolph St.
Chicago, IL 60601
Ph. 312-744-8925
www.gallery37.org

Garfield Park Conservatory
300 N. Central Park Ave.
Chicago, IL 60624
Ph. 773-638-1766 ext. 20
www.garfieldconservatory.org

March of Dimes
111 W. Jackson, 22nd Floor
Chicago, IL 60604
Ph. 312-435-4007
www.marchofdimesillinois.org

Museum of Science & Industry

57th St. and Lake Shore Dr.
Chicago, IL 60603
Ph. 773-684-1414
www.msichicago.org

Off the Street Club

25 N. Karlov
Chicago, IL 60624
Ph. 773-533-3253
www.otsc.org

PAWS Chicago

3516 W. 26th St.
Chicago, IL 60623
Ph. 773-935-PAWS or
773-521-1408 ext. 1
www.pawschicago.org

Prevent Blindness

500 East Remington Road
Schaumburg, IL 60173
Ph. 847-843-2020
www.preventblindness.org/il

Ronald McDonald House

One Kroc Dr.
Oak Brook, IL 60523
Ph. 630-623-7048
www.rmhc.com

Shedd Aquarium

1200 S. Lake Shore Dr.
Chicago, IL 60605
Ph. 312-692-3309
www.sheddnet.org

Starlight Children's Foundation

30 E. Adams, Suite 1020
Chicago, IL 60603
Ph. 312-251-7827
www.starlightmidwest.org

The Cradle

2049 Ridge Ave.
Evanston, IL 60201
Ph. 847-475-5800
www.cradle.org

The Gus Foundation

833 W. Wrightwood Ave.
Chicago, IL 60614
Ph. 773-281-5560
www.gusfoundation.org

Today's Chicago Woman Foundation

150 E. Huron St., Suite 1001
Chicago, IL 60611
Ph. 312-954-7600
www.todayschicagowoman.com

Girl Scouts

420 5th Ave.
New York, NY 10018
Ph. 1-800-478-7248
www.girlscouts.org

HighSight

1107 N. Orleans
Chicago, IL 60601
Ph. 312-787-9824
www.highsight.org

Inner City Teaching Corps

3141 W. Jackson
Chicago, IL 60612
Ph. 773-265-7240
www.ictc-chicago.org

Inspiration Café/ Inspiration Corporation

4554 N. Broadway, Suite 207
Chicago, IL 60640
Ph. 773-878-0981
www.inspirationcorp.org

Jr. League of Chicago

1447 N. Astor St.
Chicago, IL 60610
Ph. 312-664-4462
www.jlchi.org

Juvenile Diabetes Research Foundation Illinois

500 N. Dearborn St. Suite 305
Chicago, IL 60610
312-670-0313
www.jdrfillinois.org

Lambs Farm

14245 W. Rockland Rd.
Libertyville, IL 60048
Ph. 847-362-4636
www.lambsfarm.com

Lincoln Park Zoo

2200 N. Cannon Dr.
Chicago, IL 60614
Ph. 312-742-2124
www.lpzoo.com

Little City Foundation

1760 W. Algonquin Rd.
Palatine, IL 60067
Ph. 847-358-5510
www.littlecity.org

Lydia Home

4300 W. Irving Park Rd.
Chicago, IL 60641
Ph. 773-736-1447
www.lydiahome.org

Lynn Sage Cancer Research Foundation

676 N. St. Clair, Suite 2050
Chicago, IL 60611
Ph. 312-926-4274
www.lynnsage.org

Today's Chicago Woman Foundation

150 E. Huron St., Suite 1001
Chicago, IL 60611
Ph. 312-954-7600
www.todayschicagowoman.com

WINGS

P.O. Box 95615
Palatine, IL 60095
Ph. 847-963-8910
www.wingsprogram.com

YMCA

www.ymca.net

Y-ME National Breast Cancer Organization

203 N. Wabash, Suite 1220
Chicago, IL 60601
Ph. 312-364-9071
www.y-me.org/illinois

Volunteer RESOURCES
in the City!

Chicago Volunteer.net

300 N. Elizabeth St.
Chicago, IL 60607
Ph. 312-491-7820
www.chicagovolunteer.net

Compumentor

www.itresourcecenter.org

Volunteer Match

www.volunteermatch.org

Yoga Studios

Temple of Kriya Chicago

2414 N. Kedzie Blvd.
Chicago, IL 60647
Ph. 773-342-4600
www.yogakriya.org

Om on the Range

3759 N. Ravenswood #125
Chicago, IL 60613
Ph. 773-525-YOGA (9642)
www.omontherange.net

Bikram Yoga Chicago

1344 N. Milwaukee 3rd Floor
Chicago, IL 60622
Ph. 773-395-9150
www.bycic.com

Yoga Circle

401 W. Ontario
Chicago, IL 60610
Ph. 312-915-0750
www.yogacircle.com

Chicago Yoga Center

3047 N. Lincoln Ave. Suite 320
Chicago, IL 60657
Ph. 773-327-3650
www.yogamind.com

Global Yoga and Wellness Center

1823 W. North Ave.
Chicago, IL 60622
Ph. 773-489-1510
www.globalyogacenter.com

Lincolnshire Yoga

39 Plymouth Ct.
Lincolnshire, IL 60069
Ph. 847-945-0808
www.lincolnshireyoga.bizland.com/

Yoga Now

5852 N. Broadway
Chicago, IL. 60660
Ph. 773-561-YOGA (9642)
www.yoganowchicgo.com

Yoga View

232 N. Clybourn Ave.
Chicago, IL. 60614
Ph. 773-883-YOGA (9642)
www.yogaview.com

Sweet Pea's Studio (A family Yoga Center)

3717 N. Ravenswood #213
Chicago, IL. 60613
Ph. 773-248-YOGA (9642)
www.sweatpeasstudio.com

Moksha Yoga Center

700 N. Carpenter
Chicago, IL. 60622
Ph. 312-942-9642
www.monkshayoga.com

Pilates Studios

A Body Within

3701 N. Ravenswood, Suite 204
Chicago, IL. 60613
Ph. 773-404-2412
www.abodywithin.com

Flow Inc.

2248 N. Clark St.
Chicago, IL. 60614
Ph. 773-975-7540
www.flowchicago.com

Frog Temple Pilates

1774 N. Damen Ave.
Chicago, IL. 60647
Ph. 773-489-0890
www.frogtemple.com

Body Endeavors

1528 N. Halsted
Chicago, IL. 60622
Ph. 312-202-0028
www.bodyendeavorspilates.com

Power Pilates at Equinox

900 N. Michigan Ave.
Chicago, IL. 60611
Ph. 312-335-8464
www.powerpilates.com/studio/
locations/900northmichigan.html

From the Center Pilates Studio

3047 N. Lincoln Ave. Suite 310
Chicago, IL. 60657
Ph. 773-528-1099
www.fromthecenterpilates.com

DAY SPAS

The Peninsula Spa

108 E. Superior St.
Chicago, IL. 60611
Ph. 312-573-6860
www.peninsulaspachicago.com

Channing's Day Spa

54 E. Oak St.
Chicago, IL. 60611
Ph. 312-280-1994
www.channings.com

Thousand Waves Spa for Women

1212 W. Belmont Ave
Chicago, IL. 60657
Ph. 773-549-0700
www.thousandwaves.com

Urban Oasis

12 W. Maple St. 3rd Floor
Chicago, IL. 60610
Ph. 312-587-3500
www.urbanoasis.biz

Soma Spa

3329 Vollmer Rd.
Flossmoor, IL. 60422
Ph. 708-957-4400
www.thesomaspa.com

Asha Salon and Spa

1135 N. State St.
Chicago, IL. 60610
Ph. 312-664-1600
www.ashsalonspa.com

Kaya Day Spa

112 N. May St.
Chicago, IL. 60607
Ph. 312-243-5292
www.kayadayspa.com

Spa Nordstrom

520 N. Michigan Ave.
Chicago, IL. 60611
Ph. 312-379-4300
www.nordstrom.com

Honey Child Salon and Spa

735 N. LaSalle Dr.
Chicago, IL. 60610
Ph. 312-573-1955
www.honeychildsalonandspa.com

Chicago School of Massage Therapy

Professional and Student Clinic
1300 W. Belmont Ave.
Chicago, IL. 60657
Ph. 773-880-1397
www.csmt.com

Spa Ariel

1111 S. Wabash Ave.
Chicago, IL. 60605
Ph. 312-431-1573

Exhale Mind Body Spa

945 N. State St.
Chicago, IL. 60610
Ph. 312-753-6500
www.exhalespa.com

Spa Alternatives

Mobile Spa Chicago

www.mobilespachicago.com
Ph. 847-739-3106

Home Spa Sessions

www.homespasessions.com
Ph. 630-663-4001

Gardens & Other Peaceful Places

Osaka Garden in Jackson Park

6401 S. Stony Island
Chicago, IL 60617
Ph. 312-742-PLAY (7589)
www.chicagoparkdistrict.com

Anderson Japanese Gardens

318 Spring Creek Rd.
Rockford, IL. 61107
Ph. 815-229-9391
www.andersongardens.org

Lincoln Park Conservatory

2391 N. Stockton
Chicago, IL. 60614
Ph. 312-742-7736
www.chicagoparkdistrict.com

The Morton Arboretum

4100 IL. Rt. 53
Chicago, IL. 60532
Ph. 630-968-0074
www.mortonarb.com

One Last Note

I sincerely hope that you enjoyed Get A Life! In the City® Chicago. I invite you to visit our Web site at *www.getalifeinthecity.com* for more information on events and other things to do in and around the City. Feel free to send me an email at *sheena@getalifeinthecity.com* to tell me your story or to give feedback. Thank-you for allowing me to share this information with you.

Take A Class! In the City
Notes

Get Buff! In the City

Notes

Do Good! In the City
Notes

About Get A Life! In the City

Sheena M. Jones is the CEO (with a life!) of Get A Life! In the City Communications and Pulications, Inc., located in Chicago. Her company's mission is to inspire urbanities all across the country to find and unleash their passions by taking advantage of the opportunities right in their own backyard. Get A Life! In the City®: Chicaago is the first of an entire series of Get ALife! In the City® books. Please visit www.getalifeinthecity.com for more information on other products and services including customized Get A Life! In the City® plans and books for individuals, companies and groups.